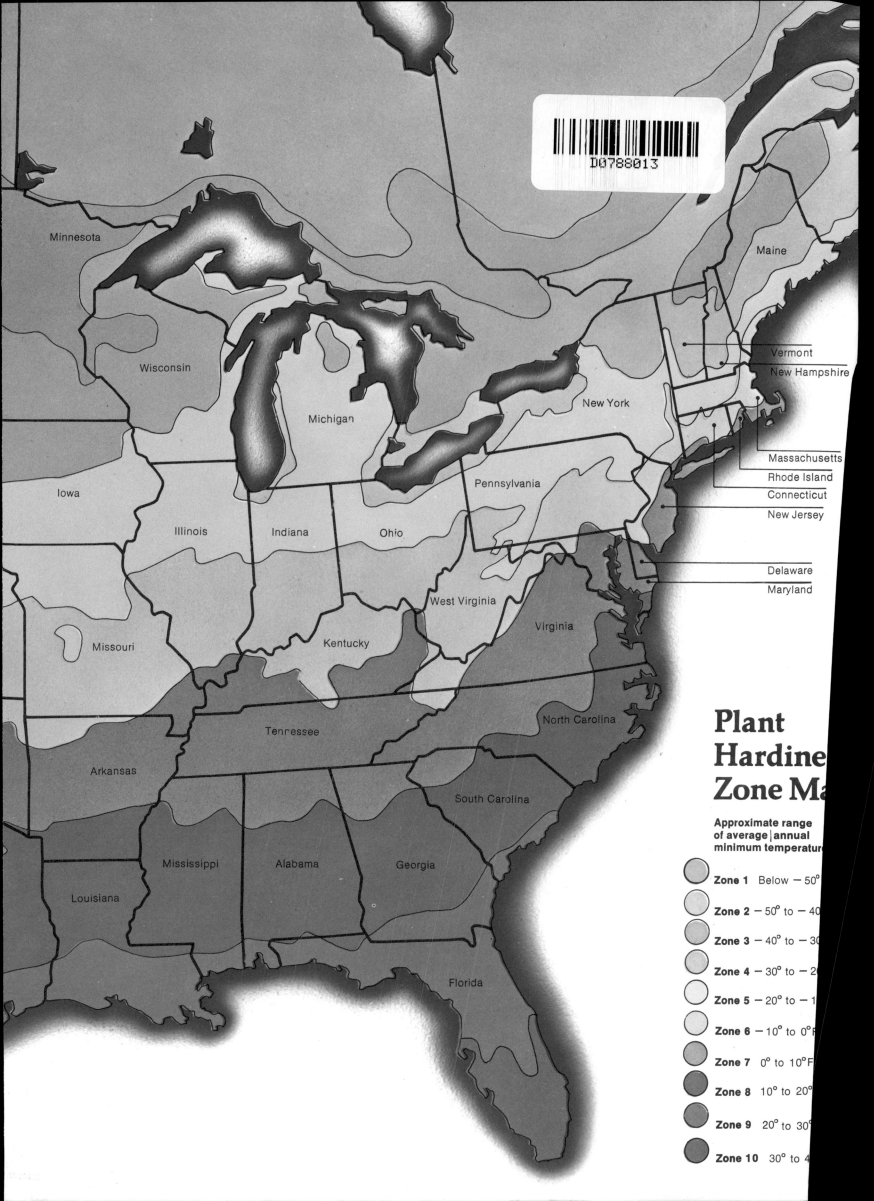

Minnesota

Maine

Wisconsin

Vermont

New Hampshire

Michigan

New York

Iowa

Massachusetts

Rhode Island

Pennsylvania

Connecticut

Illinois

Indiana

Ohio

New Jersey

West Virginia

Delaware

Maryland

Missouri

Virginia

Kentucky

North Carolina

Tennessee

Arkansas

South Carolina

Mississippi

Alabama

Georgia

Louisiana

Florida

Plant
Hardine
Zone Ma

**Approximate range
of average | annual
minimum temperatur**

Zone 1 Below − 50°

Zone 2 − 50° to − 40

Zone 3 − 40° to − 30

Zone 4 − 30° to − 20

Zone 5 − 20° to − 1

Zone 6 − 10° to 0°F

Zone 7 0° to 10°F

Zone 8 10° to 20°

Zone 9 20° to 30°

Zone 10 30° to 4

ss
ap

es

F

°F

°F

0°F

0°F

F

F

0°F

Gardening
Week by Week

Gardening Week by Week

by *Xenia Field*

Consultant Editor George H.M. Lawrence,
Director Emeritus, Hunt Botanical Library

CRESCENT BOOKS

Foreword

This is not an arbitrary or legally binding Book of Rules.

My book gives friendly advice as to how the many garden chores of the year can or might be fairly evenly spread over the weeks.

Much will depend on the size of the garden (and the gardener), the time available, and the kind of weather we have.

Some, but not all the jobs will get done, but enough of them, I hope, to give you a generous return in flowers, vegetables and fruit.

Xenia Field

Contents

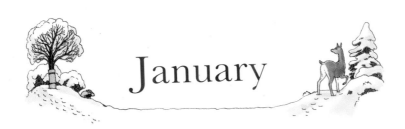

January

This is usually the coldest month of the year, which means it is the time when little can be done outdoors. The "January thaw", which generally arrives in the latter half of the month, offers no alleviation, for the ground is still frozen beneath the puddles.

If the snow is thick and deer are around, use a deer repellent to keep them from nibbling bark and buds. Deep snow means limited food for the rabbits too, so watch for any evidence of bark-feeding or, worse, stem-girdling above the snow level. Guards of wire mesh or asphalt roofing paper should be put up immediately for, once a tree has been girdled, only tedious bridge-grafting later in the year can save it.

Cultivators, mowers, shears and any tools in need of sharpening should be serviced without further delay. Tools of good, tempered steel are best sharpened on an old-fashioned, hand-turned sandstone wheel, for the heat generated by motorized, high-speed carborundum wheels will take the temper out of any edge unless great care is taken. I prefer the combination of bastard file and hand stone.

All seats, trellises, window boxes and other garden furniture brought under cover early in the winter should now be cleaned and repaired, and painted or treated with preservatives.

What were your good resolutions this year? To clean out the bottom of the hedges, weeds, leaves, debris and all? To tidy up the potting shed, wash the pots and crocks, and bundle up the stakes? Take advantage of that rare mild day and catch up on some of these chores.

Whatever your intent, do not forget to examine the begonias, dahlias, gladioli and vegetable roots for damp or rot.

A gardener can grow plants, but only a plantsman will know them. January is a good time to make yourself into a plantsman, to learn more about the plants you grow, about their discovery, introduction and idiosyncracies. Good books have been written about this heritage by David Fairchild, Alice Coats, Kenneth Lemmon, E.H. Wilson, A.W. Anderson and Tyler Whittle.

Much time has to be spent indoors during the next two months, which gives the gardener an opportunity to look after his house plants. Here are a few cultural hints to help keep them in good order.

If house plants are to survive, the dry atmosphere of homes heated by forced hot air or hot water radiators must be humidified. A humidifier with a circulating fan is fine if most of the plants are in a room that can be closed off. An alternative is to set a shallow plastic tray (the kind obtainable from auto supply stores for crankcase drippings) on a low window stand or table. Cover it with a thick layer of coarse pebbly gravel, set the plants on it and add water to a point slightly below the gravel top. The exposed surface of the wet gravel will more than double the humidity of the tray, and the system has the added advantage that the foliage can be sprayed without having to move the plants.

Spray the foliage of house plants once a day with any atomizing sprayer; even a discarded Windex bottle will do. Plants with waxy or very hairy foliage are better equipped to withstand a dry atmosphere than those that are not so well protected.

Water with care, not in rotation, but whenever the plant is thirsty (when the soil is pale-colored, the ring of the pot hollow when you tap it with stick or knuckle, and the pot light when lifted). Beware of overwatering during the winter when the plant is resting, but not even the cacti should be allowed to become desert-dry.

The plant must not be left standing in a saucer of water for any length of time.

The *Chlorophytum*, or spider plant, is indestructible and a perfect beginner's plant. Others worth trying are Swedish ivy (*Plectranthus*), wax-plant (*Hoya*), Christmas cactus and *Dieffenbachia*.

Winter-blooming Iris unguiculata prefers a poor soil and is best suited to zones 7 to 9.

January
Week 1

Garden flowers

When the ground is solid with frost, little outside work can be done for some weeks. So plan now for the renovations to be made when the season starts in earnest. Consult the new crop of catalogues for sources of the plants you want to get and study those new gardening books you got for Christmas.

Indoor plants

The gift plant: the florist or gift plant is a favorite Christmas or New Year's present. It comes straight from the greenhouse and often finds its new quarters and master quite inhospitable to its needs. Many of these plants die before they have finished flowering. They miss the even temperature, the essential humidity, and above all the professional gardener and his know-how with the watering can.

Here are tips on keeping the more popular gift plants happy.

The ubiquitous poinsettia should last through April, longer if it is a white-bracted cultivar (and pink ones last longer than reds). Today's new breeds of self-branching cultivars, such as the Hegge or Mikkelsen strains, are a great improvement on the older Ecke strains; they do not require such heavy watering and careful shelter from drafts.

Place your poinsettia in a sunny window away from the radiator, water it daily, and feed it with liquid fertilizer once a month. Continue this practice until the bracts start to fade, then reduce the water and let the plant go semi-dormant.

Plunge the pot in the garden after the last frost and bring it in again before the fall frosts. These newer varieties can be carried over much more easily than the old ones. To produce a new crop of colored bracts a poinsettia must have 16 hours of darkness daily for two months. (One sure treatment is to put it in a cupboard from 4 p.m. to 8 a.m. every day from mid-October to Christmas.)

The gloxinia goes dormant after flowering, its leaves fall and the plant looks dead. Store it on its side for a couple of months in a place where you can keep the temperature at 60°F. (15°C.). Then bring it out, water it and feed it, and new foliage will be followed by flowers.

Miniature orange and lemon trees are difficult to carry over for they require bright sun, good humidity and cool air. Feed and water them regularly and spray the foliage two or three times a week. Plunge the pot in the ground outdoors during the frost-free season.

Azaleas do best in a cool room at 60°F. (15°C.). Syringe the foliage with water weekly. Once every two weeks plunge the pot for five to ten minutes in a pail of water to which half a teaspoonful of aluminum sulphate has been added.

Open the Christmas terrarium to let air circulate through, especially if large droplets of water have collected on the sides or top. Be sure to dry the cover before replacing it.

Trees and shrubs

If snow remains a foot or more deep for an extended period, bark-girdling by small rodents becomes a probability. Undersnow tunnels are one sign of their presence and activity, so if you see one, stomp the snow down around tree trunks. Take advantage of the next thaw to install those wire or other protective guards you didn't have time to put in earlier. Most rodent damage occurs from mid- to late winter.

Where strong winds have blown off the mulch, replace it and protect it with pine boughs, boards or wire netting. Deep snow is one of the most effective mulches, but its duration is uncertain.

Greenhouse

Top ventilators (opening away from the prevailing wind) will give all the ventilation that is needed this month.

Chrysanthemums: spray or fumigate for whitefly and red spider with a nicotine or malathion insecticide.

Cyclamen should be kept on the cool side. Water daily but keep the foliage dry. If it shows signs of collapse, this will be due to lack of humidity or too warm a temperature and the plant should be promptly returned to the greenhouse. To avoid these hazards, stand the pot on moist pebbles or, better still, drop it into a larger container and fill the margin between the two containers with moss kept constantly moist.

Fertilize all actively growing pot plants on a weekly basis. Remember that, unlike clay pots, plastic pots do not absorb nutrients or moisture, so that it is easy to overfeed plants when using them. Some growers perforate their plastic pots with an electric soldering iron (when the pot is empty, of course). Feed with a liquid fertilizer such as Ra-Pid-Gro or Hyponex.

Lily of the valley pips pre-chilled for forcing can be planted now and will flower in three weeks if kept at a temperature of 75°–80°F. (24°–27°C.).

Viburnum farreri (syn. V. fragrans) presents pink apple-blossom flowers from January to April, commencing in the south and late in the north to zone 5.

January
Week 2

Garden flowers

Plan now for the coming season's planting. Send for catalogues and order the newer introductions early (for shipment at planting time), for the supply of them is often limited.

Examine dahlia stems and roots regularly and dust with Ferbam or Zeneb if there is any suspicion of mold. (These are fleshy roots, not tubers, as are potatoes.)

At the same time, check the roots to make sure they are not shriveling from being kept in too warm and dry a storage place. If dry, sprinkle lightly with water and check again in a couple of weeks. If the condition continues, store them in polyethylene bags.

Trees and shrubs

Chances are that permanent labels were not made for the new rarities you set out last year. Named cultivars and hybrids are rapidly displacing the old standard species, so it is imperative that you continue to know what you have.

A good label is inconspicuous, permanent and easily read. I prefer those made by embossing a strip of aluminum or plastic with raised block letters. They are easily made, cheap, and can be readily attached by a ring of wire or plastic. Where possible, attach them to the north side of the plant— this makes it easier to find them later.

When the January thaw arrives, spray your more tender broad-leaved evergreens with an anti-drying agent, such as Foli-Gard or Wilt-Pruf, but make sure that the temperature will be above freezing for an hour or two before and after.

Tall evergreens damaged or bent by heavy snow or ice should be straightened and retied if necessary. Replace any evergreen boughs that had been set out earlier to reduce the wind-burning of less hardy broad-leaved evergreens.

Christmas trees of pine or fir (not spruce, which loses its needles quickly) should be cut up and the branches used as mulch over bulb beds, the rock garden or the most tender evergreen ground covers.

Thoroughly soak broad-leaved evergreens planted close to the house or garage for the soil here tends to dry out, denying the shrubs the moisture they need during the windy days of the next two months.

Avoid excessive use of rock salt on walks and drives. The run-off will carry it onto lawns and other plants, killing the grass and seriously injuring trees, shrubs and perennials.

Plan to flush salt-bearing soil when the frost is out and root-feed liberally. Maples are especially sensitive to salt.

Greenhouse

Keep the schizanthus bushy by pinching back the long shoots. Stake the plants early rather than late and treat them to bi-weekly doses of liquid fertilizer.

Cuttings of ivies can be taken now and the small variegated ivies make attractive camouflage for a rubber plant that has shed its lower leaves.

Plant a pan or two of pre-chilled poetaz narcissus ('Early Perfection' and 'Allard Pierson' are good) for late February bloom. A pan of *Tulipa praestans* ('Fusilier' forces easily from pre-chilled bulbs) will produce two to four brilliant vermilion-orange flowers per stalk about five weeks from now when other indoor bulb pans are only memories. Keep at 50°–60°F. (10°–15°C.) until the first buds show color. Then raise the temperature by 10°F. (6°C.).

Watch for whitefly infestations. Christmas plants such as Jerusalem cherry, chrysanthemums and cyclamen are especially subject to this pest. Spray or dust with malathion or dimethoate and be sure to cover the under surfaces of the leaves.

Sow seeds of early-flowering sweet peas, clarkias and baby's breath for April blooming in the greenhouse, and pansies and delphiniums for the spring garden. Prick the seedlings off in a flat and put in the cold frame to harden before setting out. Some people prefer peat pots to a flat.

Grape vines can be pruned now (but not once the sap has started to flow). Prune the canes to within one or two leaf nodes of last year's growth. (For details, see December, Week 1.)

Fruit

Dwarf apple and pear trees can be pruned now. Be sure to destroy the prunings to avoid spreading insect eggs or disease spores.

Wood ashes from the fireplace contain, on average, about 32% calcium, $4\frac{1}{2}$–$5\frac{1}{2}$% potash and as much as 3% phosphoric acid, so be lavish with them around fruit tree trunks, even on the snow. They are also excellent for ivy ground cover and conifers, but avoid using them near broad-leaved evergreens.

The African violet, Saintpaulia, comes from the tropics of East Africa and enjoys steady warmth and shade from direct sunlight. It prefers a northern exposure.

January
Week 3

Garden flowers

Take advantage of the January thaw, with its run-off of melted snow, to search out the plants that have been heaved up by freezing. Resist the temptation to push them back with a heavy foot into the ground, which merely adds insult to already injured roots. Instead, cover each with a protective mulch (straw, old hay, clipped evergreen branches) and let them settle back later on their own.

Equally important, replace those short-pegged labels that have heaved completely out of the ground. If you use plastic labels, cutting a few coarse upward-cut saw teeth on each side will help to stop this.

Dahlia stems and fleshy roots should be dusted with a fungicide if there is any suspicion of mold.

Sitting in front of the fire in the evening thumbing through colorful catalogues is a chore that offers both information and delight.

My advice on making a seed list is to go first for the well-tried varieties that have served you well (but include some of the exciting novelties). When in doubt, pick from national award winners. But don't allow yourself to be carried away by the eulogies of the seedsmen.

Every gardener intent on keeping his estate gay from June until October inevitably needs some annuals and half-hardies and perhaps a special border where the flower arranger can cut ruthlessly and fancy-free. Plan for it now.

Resist the temptation to sow annuals for outdoor use too soon. Early-sown plants can become leggy and weak.

Plants that have overwintered in the cold frame must not be neglected now. Water them during any January warm spell, but be moderate. It is too early to encourage any active growth.

Shrubs

If there is a break in the winter weather, prune the espaliered shrubs, save for the roses. Cut out crossing or competing branches, bring laterals into shape and when the plant is close to the height you want, cut back the terminal shoot. Then tie and retie as needed, using stout screws and lead or wooden rawl plugs to fasten main laterals.

Espaliered or trellised roses are better pruned a month from now.

Take advantage of a mild weekend to prune dead wood out of the ornamental trees. Cut each limb close and flush to the trunk, undercutting it first from below.

Leave the pruning of dogwood and most shrubs until their flowering period is past.

Greenhouse

Indoor space with suitable light, humidity and growing room is always at a premium, so add only the choicest plants, ruthlessly culling out inferior ones in their favor.

Bedding double lobelia may be increased by cuttings rooted in light soil. (The single lobelia is best raised from seed.)

The amaryllis is encouraged into growth by warmth and watering. This bulbous plant must surely be the most showy, dramatic and fast growing we have, with its stout stalk of from three to seven tremendous lily-like flowers in crimson, scarlet and shades of pink.

The bulb can be brought into flower within a month of planting and is all but foolproof. It must be kept warm and regularly watered until it has finished growing its strap-like foliage, but when October comes it should be kept cool and dry and put to rest.

Repotting is only necessary every three years, but you should topdress the bulb annually, scraping the tired soil away and replacing it with a rich fresh loam, leaf mold and sand compost mixture.

Lilies: the ideal time to plant lilies is in the fall when the soil is still warm from the summer sun. When this cannot be done, I suggest placing them in a tray of peat to plump up, later potting them firmly in well-crocked pots half filled with top soil, leaf mold and sand (the lily has no liking for manure), afterward setting the pots in the cool greenhouse. It is a joy to bring the lilies into the house when they come into flower.

Make sure that you have enough loam, peat and washed sand for seed sowing, and *clean* seed boxes.

The bright red stems on the Cornus alba (dogwood) stand out against the winter-flowering heaths.

January
Week 4

Garden flowers

If snow cover is light or, worse, non-existent, mulch should be added to those newly worked beds and small shrubs planted in the fall. Do the same for any perennials transplanted in November. Wind-burning will come in February and March so, if you have not already done so, protect the tenderer evergreens now with pine boughs, burlap or plastic.

In zones 7 or 8, now is the time to sow sweet peas, but wait to put in California poppy seed until after the next shower.

In the warmer, more snow-free zones, lime the lawn now. If you aren't sure how much to apply, ask your local county agricultural agent for his recommendation.

Spray broad-leaved evergreens if infested with scale, as they usually are. Use a dormant oil spray as directed on the label, but only when temperature is 40° F. (4° C.) or above.

Indoor plants

Hanging baskets are back in fashion and with them the achimenes in all tones of red and pink, blue and violet.

The rhizomes may be started any time from January to April and should be planted ¾ in. deep in a free-draining, spongy compost. They do best in a temperature of 59° F. (15° C.).

Having been treated to larger pots as they are needed, the plant may finally be introduced to the hanging basket, where it mixes happily with the ivy-leaved geranium and petunias. Alternatively, several rhizomes can be grown in a 5 in. pot, thus avoiding any potting on. Always keep in a warm, light place and water with tepid water.

Make cuttings of fuchsias and heliotropes from new growth.

Even though it may be cold outside, ventilate the room regularly, even if only briefly. Freshly circulated outdoor air helps to reduce plant fungus infections.

Climbers

The usual January thaw offers a golden opportunity to prune and train most hardy climbers on walls and pergolas. Personally, I prefer to defer pruning of climbing hydrangea (including the related *Schizophragma*) until after it has flowered. Remember, climbing roses flower best on year-old canes, so cut out the darker, more aged ones 6–10 in. above the ground to generate growth for next year's blooms.

Both English and Boston ivies climb by attaching themselves with tiny roots or discoid holdfasts to their host plant or wall. The sheer weight of large masses of the vine can harm brick walls, and in time can pull apart the grouting between bricks or stones.

In no circumstances should either vine be allowed too close to the tops of active chimneys for fear of reducing air circulation through the flues.

Trees and shrubs

Gardeners looking for tub plants to place either side of the front door should consider the upright and sweet-scented rosemary, which can be gently pinched between finger and thumb as the passer-by goes in and out of the house. Start some now from cuttings.

Vines that damage trees need ruthless pruning, especially when bitter-sweet, wisteria, woodbine or English ivy become a nuisance. The first two are stranglers and, given time, will murder any live trees they grow on.

Greenhouse

Allow for a slight increase in ventilation during the middle of the day, closing down early to retain the warmth.

Gloxinias and tuberous begonias are now available. Set them in trays on moist vermiculite and pot them up once they have started in growth.

It is time now to get new growth started on the tender cultivars of English ivy. A soap-and-water bath will clean dirt from the foliage, but be sure to rinse the suds away. Then prune, feed and set in a more favorable location.

Fruit

Knobbly stubs on apple trees are often the result either of faulty pruning or attacks of woolly aphids. You can diminish the stubs gradually over two or three years by cutting the knobs back to the parent branch and painting the wound with an acceptable dressing.

Cut down newly planted summer-fruiting raspberries to within 6 in. of the ground, and be equally severe with all canes of autumn-fruiting varieties.

If there is any likelihood of rodent-girdling, cut scions now from last season's growth and store them in a bundle in a cool place, ready for bridge-grafting in late March.

Skimmia japonica berries defeat the snow. This slow-growing compact plant enjoys the shade and is hardy to zone 7.

February

Except in the warmest zones, February may well challenge January's position as the coldest month. Its average temperature is seldom noticeably higher, snowstorms are frequent and thaw periods rare. Any excess dampness can bring true misery.

But at least the days are slowly growing longer and, when the sun does begin to shine, each day is warmer than before. Early spring bulbs, especially snowdrops, may come into bloom when planted on the sunny side of a heated foundation wall.

Give constant attention to the cold frame, both to air circulation and to watering.

Plan now for the vegetable garden, and order the seeds needed. Always try some novelties, especially from last year's All-America selections, but do not discard all proven worthies until the excellence of a replacement is proven by its performance in your area. A variety that excels in New Jersey may be only so-so in Wisconsin or Maine.

Remember, the selection of vegetables should not depend only on table quality but on their ability to resist disease.

Sow your seed a smudgeon earlier than local rules-of-thumb dictate, gambling a little against the mid- to late-May frost—but be prepared to replant if you lose out.

Pruning should go forward, although there is some argument as to whether newly planted trees and shrubs should have been pruned before planting or left until March. I prefer to prune before planting, and leave only the newly planted rose bushes to be pruned later.

May I suggest that when you dive out into the garden for five to ten minutes to have a quick look around, you make a point of doing some small job— examining the soundness of a tie or the straightness of a stake, firming up a support or, on spotting a broken branch, trimming it off flush and painting the wound with a sealing paint. You'll find plenty waiting to be done.

Spray tanks should be cleaned, giving special care to the nozzle components, and light machine oil squirted on the plunger shaft. If you use chemical weedkillers, keep a separate sprayer for that purpose. These chemicals persist in the can or sprayer, and an infinitesimal quantity of a weedkiller residue can ruin a sensitive ornamental plant if the sprayer is used later for water or an insecticide.

Dormant sprays (miscible oils) may be applied to deciduous woody plants, but only when the temperature is above 45°F.(7°C.) for a few hours both before and after the application. Add ethion (Nialate®), where allowed, for better control of aphids, red spider and scale infection; be sure to penetrate bark crevices, forks and any hard-to-reach places. Two birds can be killed with one spray if Wilt-Pruf is added to the mixture (check its label for quantities) when spraying evergreens. Oil sprays may be used on fruit trees, but not beeches.

Stone fruits, flowering almonds and cherries that are suffering from leaf curl should be given a dormant spray of Ferbam® before the buds begin to green.

Mites and scale on junipers, arbor-vitae and hollies can be controlled by a miscible oil spray now or any time before growth starts. Delay spraying spruces until the buds begin to swell.

If your yews have mealybugs, an ethion-reinforced oil emulsion spray will check them, but plan to repeat the spraying in May with Meta-Systox® or malathion. The oil cuts through the insect's "wool" and contributes to its suffocation, while the ethion is a nerve poison.

A systemic insecticide added to the soil will be found effective, if a suitable one is available. Cygon® or Rogor® must only be used on plants listed on the label (not on chrysanthemums or hollies).

Snowdrops (Galanthus nivalis) appear in zone 7 at this time of year.

February
Week 1

Garden flowers

Weather permitting, rake away any accumulated debris of old leaves from under trees, beneath hedges and on the lawn. If left in place, they provide centers for root suffocation and disease, but they can usefully be added to the compost heap.

Watch now for any puddle-size wet areas of the lawn or border. Later, when all frost is out of the ground, you can fill them with sandy loam, or provide better drainage.

Trees and shrubs

Cut off and burn those thickened varnish-like bands of tent caterpillar eggs from fruit trees and ornamental shrubs, and any bagworm sacs from needle-leaved evergreens.

Destroy any black knobbly growths on ornamental cherry, peach or plum tree twigs (as well as on wild cherries in nearby hedgerows), caused by the fungus disease, black knot.

I prefer spring to the fall for planting woody ornamentals in all but the warmer zones. It gives a continuous growing season to get them established before the rigors of winter are at hand. Order now, for planting-time delivery, some of the newer cultivars of flowering dogwood and amelanchier. Try the new hardy mimosa (*Albizzia*), silver-bell and new varieties of tree peony.

Gardeners in the warmer zones can plant broad-leaved evergreens now. Apply that dormant spray, if you haven't done so already. Use it also on roses and the perennial border (if growth has not started). It is the most important spraying of the year. (For details, see preceding page.)

Also in warmer areas, transplant dormant trees and shrubs now. Take care to water well after planting. An earth rim constructed around the plant helps to retain water.

Feed sasanqua camellias as soon as they finish blooming. An azalea-type fertilizer is good for these. Prune them now.

Greenhouse

Spring always comes early to the indoor garden. With each longer day and the more warming northward transit of the sun, the greenhouse comes to life. As the growth increases, give more attention to needs of greater humidity and fresh air circulation. Where you can, spray the walk and under the bench. Better still, use a mist-nozzle installation, which can easily be installed with some high-pressure plastic tubing. Keeping each nozzle free from mineral salt deposits is the secret of success. The spray can be activated manually or, if you prefer, by an electric time-clock valve.

If you spray with aerosols, take care to keep the nozzle at least a foot away from the plant. This avoids mechanical injury. Be rash and risk overspraying rather than apply too little.

Order seeds of dwarf dahlias and semperflorens begonias for early March sowing and June or July flowering. Many new cultivars are now available and well worth trying.

Prepare a good batch of soil for sowing seed. I prefer one with equal parts of commercial potting soil, clean sand and vermiculite (or perlite), topped off with a 1 inch layer of chopped sphagnum to reduce damping off. Because most commercial potting soils have no added nutrients, add two cups of a 6-8-6 (or 5-10-5) fertilizer to each half bushel of mixture, or feed the seedlings weekly with a soluble fertilizer. (See also Week 4.)

Make cuttings now of those overgrown plants you want to have in flower again next winter: Italian bellflower, coleus, crossandra, fuchsia, geranium, heliotrope, lantana and shrimp plant.

As each will require a different amount of time for rooting, start each variety in its own pan or pot, in a mixture of equal parts of vermiculite, sand and peat moss.

Dip the lower inch of each cutting in a rooting hormone, such as Rootone, before setting it in the pot. Cover each pot with a clear plastic bag to conserve moisture and set in partial shade. Check for root growth in about ten days and transplant once the roots are about an inch long.

One of the better geraniums with tri-colored foliage is 'Mrs Henry Cox'. Its leaf colors are particularly brilliant when grown in full sun, and it makes a good pot plant in winter. Start a few cuttings now and pinch the plants to induce bushiness.

Another "goodie" for outdoor planting after the last frost, and for the greenhouse in winter, is Egyptian star-cluster (*Pentas lanceolata*) of the madder family. Its clusters of ixora-like flowers come in shades of pink to red, or in white. Grow it in full sun or half shade, as you would geraniums; its maximum height is about 15 in.

Chimonanthus praecox (syn. C. fragrans) is winter-flowering, depending upon the zone it is in, from December into March. It has very fragrant, waxy flowers.

18

February
Week 2

Garden flowers

Bring indoors, for early flowering, branches of forsythia, flowering quince, shadbush or any of the vernal witch hazels. Generally speaking, cut any spring-blooming shrub for forcing about five weeks ahead of its normal flowering time.

Plunge the branches at once in 10–14 in. of water. Leave them in a cool garage or cellar for four or five days at 40°–50° F. (5°–10° C.) before bringing into a warmer room and sunny exposure. Do not cut off the stem ends later or disturb any callus that may start to form on them.

Greenhouse

For summer bloom plant tuberous begonias any time from now until May. Prepare a flat or tray filled with equal parts of sandy loam, peat moss and vermiculite. The tubers should be set about an inch apart on this, with their top or saucer-shaped sides uppermost. Use about $\frac{1}{4}$ in. of the same mixture to cover the tops. Keep them moist but not wet, at a temperature of 61°–64°F. (16°–18° C.). If they are overwatered, remove excess water with a paper towel and return the soil over the paper.

When new growth is 2–3 in. high, transplant each plant into its own 6 in. pot of potting soil. Prune off all but the two strongest shoots. Wait until the last frost is past to set outdoors, preferably in a position that has some morning sun but offers shade thereafter. Water liberally and regularly and feed every other month.

Take stock of your house plant tools. If you keep soil mixtures in metal containers or bins, an old-fashioned sugar or grain scoop, preferably made of sheet metal, is more useful than a trowel. Have a hand tamper for compressing soil in seed pans or flats before seed sowing (never do this afterwards). Essential when repotting is a wooden rammer, which can easily be made by beveling a stick $1\frac{1}{2} \times 1 \times 12$ in. at one end. Two sizes of dibble (made from $\frac{1}{4}$–$\frac{1}{2}$ in. dowel stock) are useful when pricking off seedlings.

I like to use a glass plate (window glass) over each pot or pan of freshly sown seed. It helps to retain moisture, makes ventilation easy, lets the light in and allows you to see what's happening. Sow tiny seeds on finely chopped, slightly compacted sphagnum (you won't require a burlap layer over them). Water them with an atomizer.

Now is the time to bring in those pots or pans of perennial or ericaceous seeds you may have left out for overwinter stratification. If you can, set them over some bottom heat. Keep them moist, but not wet, while you watch for germination. Prick the seedlings into small peat pots when first true leaves are at least $\frac{1}{4}$ in. long.

When planning your spring sowing, it is vital to remember that space is essential if your plants are to grow well. Think in terms of the number of plants to be accommodated indoors before the outdoor season opens. The plants from a solitary 10 in. square seed pan will require a shelf 1 ft. wide and 6 ft. long!

If you do not have a cold frame, build yourself one now. The prefab kind are available in kit form and not too hard to assemble, even for novice carpenters. Locate your frame on a southerly exposure protected from westerly winds. Avoid any spot where snow from a roof can fall on it. Use it as an annex to the greenhouse or for direct sowing into a prepared seed-bed. It will help accommodate those extra seedlings when the greenhouse bulges—as it inevitably will.

Lawn

In the warmer zones lawn care starts now. To roll or not to roll is a moot question, but rolling is not essential.

Fertilize so that each 1,000 sq. ft. of lawn gets about 1 lb. of nitrogen, i. e. 5 lb. of a 20-10-5 mixture, or 10 lb. of a 10-6-4. Apply *before* growth starts. Merion blue grass is a voracious feeder and particularly strong grower, so if you have a blue grass lawn you will need to use twice the recommended quantity of fertilizer. Although the initial cost is higher, the increased gains from using a slow-release ureaform fertilizer (formula: about 22-18-20) truly justify the expense. Why? One application is enough for the entire season because the nutrients dissolve slowly as needed. When it is properly applied, the risk of turf-burning is nil.

For crab grass control use a pre-emergence weedkiller, either with the fertilizer or separately. Local garden nursery shops all carry selective sprays to kill weeds such as dandelion and plantain.

Take the time to reseed bare spots now, or you will reap weed patches later.

A frequently mowed lawn is always healthier than one that is allowed to grow tall between mowings. The freshly cut tender crowns of grass plants are damaged by being exposed to hot sun, and brown patches can result.

Cyclamen persicum in full bloom in the greenhouse.

February
Week 3

Garden flowers

Violets and pansies in cold frames will appreciate it if you lift or remove the sash on mild days.

In warmer areas a lily of the valley bed can be started in semi-shade. If your soil is heavy with clay, mix in leaf mold, sand and vermiculite. In more northern zones prepare and plant as soon as the ground is friable.

Once the soil has dried out enough, prepare a similar bed for the hardy chrysanthemums.

Protect plants in the rock garden from frost-heaving damage by adding a non-compacting mulch. Even a bale of chicken litter from a local feed store will do if your own mulch supply is exhausted. The plant will greatly prefer being mulched to having a heavy foot stomped on it!

Shrubs and trees

Offer the broad-leaved evergreens a second application of an anti-dessicant, such as Foli-Gard or Wilt-Pruf, especially if there has been more rain than snow in recent weeks. This is particularly helpful for those shrubs that went on producing new growth well into the fall, or were planted too late to make new root growth.

Complete all pruning of ornamental and fruit trees so that you can give your full attention to the sowing and planting program that you will soon have in hand.

Climbers

Pruning clematis is confusing for beginners but, to simplify the undertaking, species that flower on the current year's growth, such as the viticella types and the late-flowering paniculata type, should be cut back to within 12 in. of the base in February or early March.

The large-flowered Jackmanii hyrids, including the popular 'Pink Chiffon' or 'Comtesse de Bouchard' and the double and semi-double forms such as 'Duchess of Edinburgh', which flower on the previous year's wood, should be kept in place but only lightly pruned. Weak wood may be thinned out and the growths left shortened to a strong pair of buds.

Clematis root rot (wilt) occurs near the soil surface and has no known cure. Best bet is to spray the foliage with Captan once before flowering and again soon afterward, and pray.

Two very hardy Jackmanii types (unrelated, with flowers 2 in. across) are hybrids of *C. alpina* by *C. macropelta*. One cultivar is sold as *C. alpina* 'Pamela Jackman' and has pure blue flowers. Another, named 'Ruby', has rose-red flowers in more of a bell shape.

Greenhouse

Delphinium seed sown now will produce plants of flowering size by mid-September. As soon as four to six leaves are present, harden off in the cold frame. Wait until mid-April to plant out, however. Seeds offered in the Pacific Northwest, or by Blackmore and Langdon in England, usually give the best plants.

Watch the geranium cuttings and discard any showing the fatal signs of black rot.

The longer warmer days are an invitation to carelessness in the greenhouse. Maintain the humidity, but ventilate enough to avoid too high a midday temperature.

Fruit

If a tree is suffering badly from disease, it is better grubbed up and burned, where possible. It is a mistake to turn your garden into a nursing home.

Canker can be spread from one tree to another, even by pruning tools. If a limb is severely affected, it should be ruthlessly removed (and the wound dressed) rather than disfigured by a series of incisions.

Eastern red cedar (*Juniperus virginiana* and relatives) is the alternate host of cedar rust on apples, cherries and stone fruits. Ideally, all cedars within 100 yards of such plants should be exterminated. Take pains to remove and destroy any vestiges of the rust on cedars that cannot be cut down.

General

Repair and paint the trellises brought in last November. If you use clear wood preservatives in lieu of paint, the copper-based type (such as Cupranol) will cause less harm to a plant than kinds made from creosote. Cupranol is also available as a clear (not green) liquid.

The so-called redwood or shingle stains all contain opaque pigments and will "chalk" in time, which makes the unpigmented clear preservatives preferable.

Ilex aquifolium, a red-berried holly with spiny leaves edged with yellow.

February
Week 4

Garden flowers

Spring has come to the southern zones and will soon spread its color northwards. The earliest of spring bulbs are flowering now: snowdrops and the eranthis or aconite, the earliest of the crocus species. The green spears of daffodil foliage show themselves here and there.

The bright days of late February can be unseasonably warm, causing some plants to start new growth prematurely. Such days are as dangerous as late frosts, and harder to cope with.

Watch now, or maybe a little later, for the early emergence of the foxtail or candle lily (*Eremurus*). When that stout shoot pushes through, be ready to protect it with mulch if it shows up before late March, or a hard freeze will ruin it. I use an inverted old bushel basket over such upstarts, breaking a hole in the bottom to leave room for later tip growth.

Chrysanthemums: avoid the beginner's pitfall of planting your first mum in the fall—container-grown, in full bloom, it is likely to be dead by spring. Instead, read the catalogues now. Study the pictures.

Buy rooted cuttings of a dozen kinds and grow them on in the greenhouse. Shape the plants by pinching off first the center bud, later the laterals. Feed well. Shift them once only to 5 in. pots. Let them harden off in the cold frame, but wait until early May to set them out.

These plants should be dug and divided in early spring of every year. Be ruthless and keep only the outer, more vigorous shoots. Or, if you prefer, propagate by cuttings from those shoots.

Shrubs

Recheck the protective measures you gave to individual broad-leaved evergreens. Secure any dislodged evergreen boughs, or unfurled burlap or plastic, especially when protecting plants that are in full sun or that were planted last fall. The combination of full sun, March winds and dried-out soil can do horrifying damage to roots and foliage in a very short period of time.

Keep young trees free from grass and weeds at the base. Once the soil's surface is exposed, enrich it with a good dressing of rotted organic matter. If you haven't any, use Milorganite. The trees will enjoy either.

The buddleias or butterfly bushes, in particular, respond to severe pruning. Even in warmer zones cut them back to last year's wood and they will put out vigorous new growth with abundant bloom. In zone 5 (their northern limit) they usually winter-kill to the mulch line (a foot or so above soil level), but send up new flower shoots in profusion later.

If winter has been severe in zone 5 or northward, exposed plants of firethorn (*Pyracantha*) will benefit from whatever protection you can give them now against the drying winds of March.

Greenhouse

There is a long time gradient from zone 8 in the south and zone 5 in the north, over which chrysanthemum crowns begin to send up new growth. In those areas where such growth is now 2–3 in. high, make cuttings of the cultivars you want for your new stock.

I like a more sandy mixture for chrysanthemums than for geraniums or carnations because it makes it easier to control disease.

Seed pans of aluminum with perforated bottoms are fine (salvage frozen food pans from the kitchen, or buy them new at the supermarket). Using smaller ones reduces the spread of disease and allows you to be more flexible in mixing soil and handling seedlings. Fill only to within ½ in. of the top.

Some growers prefer a sterile soilless mixture of vermiculite and peat, such as Pro-Mix or Jiffy-Mix. If you use this, enrich it by feeding with some form of fertilizer.

Soil mix for seed pans should be treated with Captan ® dust (¼ oz. per sq. ft.), well mixed before sowing, or drenched lightly after sowing with Captan (1 tablespoon per gallon of water), 1 pint per sq. ft. Repeat at five-day intervals. (See also Week 1.)

The seed should be sown as thinly as possible to avoid damping off. Very small seeds, such as the gloxinia, should be placed on the surface of the soil and only lightly covered with sand; the larger seeds, including the nasturtium and lupin, are better covered with soil from the sieve ¼ in. deep, then sprinkled lightly with sand. Finally, water the seed with a fine rose-can and leave the container to drain. Cover the pan or box with glass and paper. Most seeds germinate best in darkness (lettuce being a notable exception).

The soil must be kept slightly moist until the seedlings appear.

Half-hardy (i. e. frost-tender) annuals are normally raised from sowings made in a warm greenhouse from early February until the end of April. They call for more attention than the hardy ones, and success depends greatly on acclimating them to outdoor conditions (hardening them off) without impeding their growth.

The half-hardy annuals complete their life cycle within the space of a season. If the gardener has neither greenhouse nor frame, he can sow outdoors in late March (but be sure to wait until April in the northern and colder districts).

Male catkins of a showy pussy willow, for March and April bloom.

March

The weather varies more in March than in any other month of the year. Gardeners in the north must take into account the time lag caused by the colder temperatures before starting to sow. In northern zones where the temperature may still fall to below 18°F. (–8°C.), plants and even turf will wait until April before growing.

March is a fickle month, when the garden stirs fitfully from its winter's sleep, and often takes a second nap under an unexpectedly heavy blanket of snow. Keep an eye on Nature's mood rather than relying on the calendar. In some years the work suggested here for March cannot possibly be done until April!

Only in the more southerly zones is it safe to uncover the roses or take mulch from the bulb beds. Again, follow Nature, not the calendar.

Watch early for crocuses and snowdrops to poke through the soil, and remove their mulch cover if their growth is distorted.

In the southern zones, borders can be tidied up, stems cut down and the soil top-dressed with a good fertilizer, such as Milorganite or a 6-8-8 mix. Apply at a rate of 4 lb. per 100 sq.ft. This can be done while the ground is still frozen.

If there are gaps to fill, the budget will dictate the choice: a packet of seed of dwarf marigold, candytuft or 'Dwarf Jewel' nasturtium will meet the need, but if a tree peony can be afforded then glamour will be added to the border.

In the north, be guided by the friability (crumbliness) of the soil. Remember that there will still be exposures and pockets where it remains solid with ice and frost. If the season is early, pussy willows will be out, Dutch crocuses will show some color, and snowdrops and eranthis will be in full bloom.

Add ground limestone to the flower beds if the soil tests a pH of 5.0 or below (but not near ericaceous or other acid-soil plants). If you are using hydrated lime, halve the quantity and do *not* apply it along with the fertilizer.

Among the first plants to be set out are the pansies. After their first flush of growth, if you pinch them back regularly and keep the blossoms picked, they will go on flowering for many weeks.

Sow sweet peas as early as the soil permits—by mid-March in zone 6, earlier further south. Preparing the soil for them in advance brings rich rewards. Mix well-rotted manure to a depth of 4–6 in. in a trench twice as wide, and compact firmly. Then make a furrow 2 in. deep, sow the seed half an inch beneath it, and fill the trench gradually as the plants develop.

Remember to retrieve the lawn mowers and other power tools sent away for overhaul.

The gardener should now give his attention to interesting and attractive flower associations: the painter's palette is in his hand, and it is for him to see that every group and drift of flowers enhance each other.

Many of our annuals deserve exciting companions, among them the splendid little lobelia condemned for generations to be the inevitable bedfellow of scarlet geranium and white alyssum. This brilliant small flower, available in a choice of new cultivars, should be planted in blocks and drifts rather than in institutional lines, and will play an important part in a blue border along with phacelia, nemophilia and love-in-the-mist, with delphiniums in the background.

Not everybody has the space for a blue border, but there is always room for a blue patch. I once filled my window box with Cambridge lobelia: it was long-lasting, trouble-free and truly beautiful.

Plantings depend on taste. There are those who go for pale shades, and a pale planting with a backing of becoming green foliage is delightful. But there are others who prefer the garish and would enjoy a border of red and orange such as I saw once long ago, so brilliant that even the thought of it makes me blink.

Spring flowers.

March
Week 1

Garden flowers

Decide now if you will grow annuals and perennials from plants bought at local garden centers or shopping plazas, or from your own choice of seed. The former will usually provide good plants of older time-tested cultivars, whereas the latter open the door to a wide range of new introductions, including recent All-America winners. I prefer the second choice, knowing the other is at hand if need be.

If you elect to raise your own annuals, do not sow them too early. Now is the time for starting slow-growing lobelias, alyssum, begonias, dahlias and salvias, but leave the petunias, nemesias, snapdragons and marigolds until early April, otherwise they are apt to get leggy and outstay their time in greenhouse or cold frame.

As a precaution against later blasting of peony buds, spray the ground above them with any good fungicide, such as Ferbam or Zineb. Once the shoots reach 2–3 in., repeat the treatment twice at ten-day intervals.

Greenhouse

Pot up rooted cuttings of geraniums, mums and fuchsias, using a mixture of equal parts of fibrous loam, well-rotted manure, leaf mold and sand. For each 3 gallon pailful add a cup of 5-8-6 fertilizer. Water the plants moderately for the first ten days. Keep a sharp lookout for whitefly and dust with malathion at the first sign of it.

Seed sowing starts in earnest this month.

Make ready your planting lists for ornamentals and vegetables, and the pans, boxes (flats) and labelling supplies you will need. The more nearly sterile the receptacles, the fewer will be the problems with disease.

If you only need a couple of pails of soil, a sealed bag of prepared sterilized mixture should be bought. This reduces the spread of disease and saves time. Even so, keep a smaller bag of sterile chopped sphagnum and one of vermiculite at hand so that you can modify the mixture for special needs: sphagnum to provide the top layer on which every fine seed must be sown, vermiculite for the added water retention needed by some slow-germinating perennials.

Compress the soil before you start sowing to a level about 3–4 in. below the container edge. Cover the seed with sieved soil to a depth twice the thickness of the seed (seed sown on sphagnum needs no covering) and label with name and sowing date. Avoid sowing fast- and slow-germinating seed in the same pot or flat.

It is essential to maintain soil moisture throughout the germination period by watering carefully with a fine spray. Moisture can be retained by covering the soil with a moist paper towel; I prefer setting a glass plate on top of the container edges. A daytime air temperature of 54°–61°F. (12°–16°C.) is needed. Temperatures should not drop more than 10°F. (−12°C.) at night.

Shrubs

Dormant roses can be planted out now, if the soil is not too wet (if a handful stays in a ball after squeezing, it *is* clearly too wet). Check whether the stems have been clearly waxed by the grower and, if not, mound the earth around them to a depth of about a foot to reduce drying-out. Such early planting will encourage root growth several weeks ahead of new shoot growth and more flowers this season.

When should roses be pruned? Rosarians differ in their answers but it is largely a matter of which hardiness zone you are in. In zones 7 and 8, mid-winter is the preferred time. In areas farther north, I prune in the fall, burning the prunings, then check again after the winter mulch is removed, pruning away any winter-killed wood. The farther south one lives, the shorter the rose bush's productive life. The maximum in zone 8 may be three years, as against one year in zone 9.

The aim of rose pruning is to keep the bush open to light and air, dismissing dead and crossing canes and weak wood. If a whole plant is weak, be strong-minded and grub it out.

Vegetables

Plan your outdoor layout in advance. Rototill if the size of your garden warrants it, adding lime in advance as needed and organic mulch as available.

Indoors sow seed of cabbage, cauliflower and broccoli.

Dress asparagus beds with any high-nitrogen lawn fertilizer. The ureaform slow-release types are ideal.

Cut pea brush now (from wild birch where available) for later use. The branches will make more effective vine supports if you flatten them under boards.

Eranthis tubergeniana, the winter aconite, prefers growing under trees and is colony-forming.

March
Week 2

Garden flowers

Once the soil is friable, prepare beds or spots in the border for divisions of autumn-flowering perennials. Old crowns of asters, mums, balloon flowers and Japanese anemones can be divided and replanted.

Gaps in the perennial garden may be filled with early flowering annuals; permanent replacements can follow when available. Cleome, 'Pink Queen' petunia and nicotiana seed should be sown now. Properly hardened-off seedlings can be set out six weeks later.

Trees and shrubs

Feed the trees as soon as frost is out of the ground. With sledge and crowbar make holes 12–18 in. deep (less deep for maples and beeches than for oaks, magnolias or willows), keeping them about 2 ft. apart over the area covered by the branches. Fill with a 6-8-7 or similar fertilizer and cap with a handful of soil.

Feed deciduous shrubs with the same fertilizer, spreading it liberally over the ground beneath the branches.

Use an azalea-type fertilizer for the broad-leaved evergreens. If the foliage looks yellowish, supplement with chelated iron, aluminum sulphate or another acidifying agent, following the instructions on the label. Ammonium nitrate will be found especially effective in correcting yellowing; extra nitrogen is also helpful.

Deciduous hedges can be planted in well-prepared ground during a mild spell.

In northern zones where buds have yet to open, it is still not too late to spray with dormant oil. For control of aphids, scale insects and mites, add ethion (Nialate®). This spray can be used on evergreens and most deciduous woody plants (but *not* on maples, magnolias, beeches or nut trees). Remember, the dormant spray is the most important one of the year.

Prune dead wood from deciduous shade trees and open up their crowns (but, if the sap has begun to flow, do not prune maples).

Plant new trees and shrubs, including dogwoods, redbuds, magnolias, birches and cherries as soon as the soil is in suitable condition. Tulip trees do not transplant well, and tree peonies are equally difficult. They should be wholly dormant, and the smaller the plants the less likely you are to lose them.

Lawn

One of two situations will usually confront you now: the need to renovate an old lawn or to establish a new one. Wait until late summer if it is to be returfed or resown.

Renovation will fill in the bare spots where turf has been killed by disease or winter conditions, or has been overrun with weeds. A new seedbed will be required for each spot. First, dig up the bad area. Lime if need be (but not if a bent-grass is to be used). Feed with a high-nitrogen lawn fertilizer that includes a weedkiller. Then seed with either a mixture or a single selection. Blue grass is the easiest grass to establish, while fescues do best in shady areas.

Bent grasses produce the finest turf but require high summer humidity (achieved by the magic of mechanical watering or ocean fogs) and acid soil. (See August, Week 3.)

Small areas are best handled by sodding with commercial turf, but this can be costly.

Every lawn needs feeding about now (even earlier in southern zones) with a high-nitrogen lawn fertilizer. If crab grass is a problem, select one with a pre-emergence killer to cope with that pest and most broad-leaved weed seedlings.

Vegetables

Spread a good handful of a lawn fertilizer, or some rotted manure, around each rhubarb plant. Growth is wanted and is the main reason for feeding.

An asparagus bed, well maintained, will go on producing for many years, but it takes three years to bring a bed into production. The earliest crops come from those on sandy soils. Plant three-year crowns of 'Mary Washington' in furrows 1 ft. deep and 5 ft. apart, the crowns 2 ft. apart in the row. Cover with 3–4 in. of soil, and fill in gradually as the season advances.

Fruit

Bridge-graft any girdled trees, using graft wood saved from earlier pruning. Space the grafts about 2 in. apart.

Set out new trees as soon as the soil is friable.

Prune currants and gooseberries, if you have them. But note that these can be grown only in areas where the law permits, because they are alternate hosts for white pine blister rust.

Crocus tomasinianus, the silvery lilac species, is early flowering and hardy into zone 6.

March
Week 3

Garden flowers

Check mulched beds and borders for signs of bulb-sprouting beneath the mulch and remove the dressing from those showing 3–4 in. of new growth.

Where snowdrop flowering is over, divide heavy clumps and replant. It is better that they be lifted when green and growing than when dormant. Divide daffodils where needed. Retain only the best sorts and naturalize the others.

Set out forget-me-nots among the rose bushes.

Cannas, in warmer zones, can now be set out in the open. The newer, very dwarf ones make fine occupants for tubs or window boxes, but watch them for they will not tolerate drying-out.

A second sowing of sweet peas can certainly be made now in zones 7 and 8, and with slight risk in zone 6. Have you tried the newer bush types, which need no supports, and range from dwarf to 15 in.? 'Bijou Pinkette' and 'Bijou Scarlette' are both international award winners.

Shrubs

Espaliered roses (and those on trellises) require renewal of the primary canes to ensure new year-old canes for strong flowering. Untie the canes and lay them on the ground, cutting out the older stems, which are usually darker colored, to achieve a 1 ft. spacing on the wall or trellises. Retie them, and prune the tops to below desired height.

Experiment, and use other materials to espalier your walls. Forsythia or firethorn (pyracantha) is an excellent choice, and so is flowering quince (although slower growing). If you have sufficient space, wisteria is marvellously rewarding.

Ground cover, like other plantings, requires feeding now. If the growth is dense, use a liquid fertilizer when the weather is cloudy.

Greenhouse

Check the earlier sowings of annuals, and when at least two true leaves are showing, prick off the seedlings into pressed-peat or flats of potting mixture.

Sow the seeds of the more tender annual flowers and vegetables: zinnias, verbenas, China asters, ageratums, annual phlox (*P. drummondii*) and the new 'Imp' strain of impatiens. Sow three or four seeds of the newer cultivars of morning glory, moonflower and *Cobaea scandens* in individual 3 in. pots.

Sow peppers, tomatoes and eggplants indoors.

Now is the time to start canna roots. You can save precious greenhouse space by planting them in earth in boxes 6–8 in. deep and leaving them in the cellar until the new growth is 6 in. high. Bring them into the light in a place free from frost, then harden them off in a frame and plant them out in early May.

Start dahlia roots in pots. When the shoots are 3–4 in. high, cut off a few and root them in the cutting box (in shade). These will become next winter's carry-overs.

Repot the azalea you were given last winter by replacing the tired peat and earth from the root ball and returning the plant to the same pot with new soil. Cut the plant back slightly, place it in full sun and water well. Remember to spray for red spider.

House plants should be repotted now to produce vigorous new growth during spring and summer. To hold a plant to its present size, prune and replant in the same pot, as with the azaleas. Old fuchsias often benefit by having enough soil removed to fit the next smaller size pot. But remember to trim the branches as well as the roots!

Young fuchsias should go into 4 in. pots. Water them well, and after a few days feed with a liquid booster such as Ra-Pid-Gro. Pinch back and shape as growth develops.

Many fuchsias fall by the wayside through irregular attention with the can. Regular watering, not occasional sprinkling, should be the order of the day.

Vegetables

Plant onion sets, shallot bulbs and garlic kernels now.

Sow lettuce in an outdoor seedbed for future transplanting. Sow radishes, parsley, beets and chard in rows. Cover very lightly to keep the lettuce seed from drying out. Sow peas in a prepared trench, as described earlier for sweet peas.

Fruit

Strawberry beds should be uncovered with caution, and any plants lifted by frost gently pressed back into place. A layer of straw covering may be kept between the rows for the berries to rest on.

In warmer zones set out the new strawberry bed (a two- to three-year rotation is ideal), with plants 16–18 in. apart in rows 2 ft. apart.

Dwarf fruit trees have much in their favor. When planting, keep the graft union a few inches above ground level or the dwarf character of the tree may be lost.

Crocus chrysanthus with striking orange-scarlet stigmata. The leaves are long, keeled and very narrow.

March
Week 4

Garden flowers

The yellow-flowered winter aconite (*Eranthis*) is now past its glory. When happy, it seeds itself freely. It should be given a bonemeal dressing, followed in the fall with a taste of Milorganite.

Make plans to plant some Christmas roses (*Helleborus niger*) in a shady spot too moist for many other plants. Plant out next month, using an enriched woodsy soil, for this customer is a lime-hater. (For other varieties, see December.)

Shrubs

Trees and shrubs, arriving from the nursery when weather conditions do not permit planting, are quick to dry out; they must be soaked in a bucket of water before planting. Heel them in for the time being if it is too early to plant them permanently.

Deciduous shrubs will appreciate a mulch of mixed shredded manure and compost. Most newcomers benefit by being given a generous amount of peat mixed in with the soil; there *are* peat-haters (such as lilacs and peonies), but they are in a minority.

In southern zones, the exotic passion flower should be thinned out. If doing poorly, nematodes may have infected the roots, in which case they should be drenched with Nemagon. Weak shoots should be removed and strong ones shortened by one third.

It is time to feed japonica camellias, of which some newer cultivars are now hardy as far north as Long Island (see October, Week 2).

A feed of any good azalea fertilizer will be appreciated.

Camellia plants are hardy: it is the flower buds of the camellia, not the plant, that suffer from frost damage. It is largely to protect the buds that the plants are winter-wrapped. The japonicas are hardier than sasanquas, which often bloom in November, before the buds are frozen.

The weeds that grow so luxuriantly beneath the hedge may be kept down with pre-emergence weedkillers now, and by careful close spraying in June with an approved herbicide.

Overgrown deciduous hedges can be cut back hard to within a foot of the ground, and afterwards fertilized. Yew hedges that have gotten out of hand need cutting back severely. They will send out new growth and will be fully "recovered" by July.

Heaths (*Erica* spp.) and heathers (*Calluna vulgaris* cvs.) are layered easily in March. Scarify or slit the lower side of a few branches and peg each branch down into a mound of sand-peat-loam. This soil mixture should be kept moist, but not wet.

Remove the mulch from *Hydrangea macrophylla* (the pink or blue hortensia type), and prune out all dead wood. Prune *H. paniculata* hard, at least a third of its growth, in order to have vigorous growth for this year's bloom (see June, Week 3).

Prune out wood of snow- or wind-damaged plants. Winter-killed privet must be cut back to live wood, even to 2–3 in. stubs when damage is severe.

Watch for winter-killing of ground covers such as English ivy; remove old growth and, if necessary, replace with one of the newer, more hardy cultivars.

Greenhouse

Ventilation is made difficult by winds; beware of drafts and only use top ventilators, unless the temperature jumps up at a suspicion of sun.

Heliotrope cuttings rooted in sandy soil will be ready for June planting. Crop the leaves and shade for the first few days.

Repot the Boston, maidenhair, bird's-nest and other ferns, mixing an extra handful of chopped sphagnum in the soil.

Fuchsias should be pinched back regularly. Use the prunings as cuttings if you need more plants.

Sow herbaceous perennials in the cold frame or greenhouse, covering the seeds with finely sieved soil. Shade from sunlight until germinated.

Some annuals make fine pot plants; among them are the double stocks which give a drench of fragrance.

Stake and tie growing plants early rather than late. Schizanthus needs regular training.

House plants can be restarted into growth by judicious watering and a little more heat.

Feeding can begin once the plants show new growth, but never feed when the soil is dry or the plant in bad health or resting; most plants rest in the winter from September to April. Overfeeding is a temptation; the manufacturer's instructions should be followed, or you will be in trouble. Give a little less rather than more, and no double doses. The meanest of men becomes madly generous with the fertilizer container.

The schizanthus should be potted on before it becomes rootbound.

Fruit

Where space is limited set a few *Fraises des Bois* (French woodland strawberries). Smaller than market berries, their flavor is intense, and they are juicier and sweeter. Plant 1 ft. apart in the flower border or in a bed; give them ordinary soil, but keep it damp. The cultivar 'Charles V' is stolonless, prolific and ever-bearing.

Chinese andromeda, shown flowering in zone 7.

April

This is the month of hope and anticipation.

Warm sunshine is invariably followed by frost at night and should you be caught napping late in the month and a rare plant frozen, it should be thawed by spraying with tepid water from the watering can, covering it afterwards with paper or black plastic. April is another month when the gardener must be guided not by books, but by Nature in bringing plants into bloom.

If weather conditions hold back the bloodroot, hepatica, shadbush or marsh marigold and make them late, you must slow down too.

Much time this month will be spent in sowing seed and hardening off seedlings. Hardening off (acclimating seedlings to the cooler outdoor conditions before planting out) should begin at an early stage.

As you work in the garden, watch where you step or scuff with the hoe. Brave young tips of lilies, peony or hibiscus can easily be damaged.

Have a sample of your garden soil tested, either by soil kit or at your state experimental station, and improve the soil as the tests dictate.

Eyesores can be screened cheaply with such fast-growing vines as the Madeira vine (*Boussingaultia*), cinnamon vine (*Dioscorea batatas*), hops or even the hyacinth bean (*Dolichos lablab*).

Bulbs of some lilies planted now will flower this year. Try the regal lily, or any of Jan de Graff's *auratum* by *speciosum* hybrids. Discard those Easter lily bulbs; they often carry virus diseases and pass them on to other lilies.

It pays to use a liquid fertilizer when transplanting trees, shrubs or perennials. I add it to the water in which I drench or puddle them. It will promptly improve the foliage color of broad-leaved evergreens. Some growers soak the seed furrows with a starter solution just before sowing.

This is the month to plant such shrubs as mountain laurel, calycanthus, viburnum, magnolia, rose of Sharon, dogwood, pyracantha, lilac, clematis and philadelphus. Use container-grown or balled and burlaped stock whenever possible.

Lilac and clematis need lime. Work it into the soil to a depth of 4 in. and a radius of 18 in. around the base of the plant. Lilacs will grow better if the grass is kept away from their base. Clematis *Jackmanii* hybrids should be planted with the crown 2–3 in. below the surface.

May I remind the novice spring-cleaning the herbaceous border that the peony, scabious and the *Alstromeria* hybrids should be left strictly alone; they resent disturbance and demonstrate their feelings by sulking. Bearded iris are happier when moved and divided after flowering.

Rampant growers should be severely controlled, in particular the aggressive cerastium, golden alyssum, rudbeckia and saponaria.

Seedlings must be pricked out before they jostle each other, otherwise they will grow tall and spindly, and never fully recover.

Now to the greenhouse, where the schizanthus should be soon at the top of its form with the calceolarias not far behind.

The temperature must not be allowed to rise above 64°F. (18°C.). Ventilate the house in the morning, closing up at about 4 p.m.

Frame sashes may be lifted a little higher every day until they can be removed altogether. If the seedlings change color, or stop growing, beware!

Nearly all greenhouse plants can be propagated this month, and the pot-bound will be crying for attention.

The time for sowing in the open ground will depend on the weather; it is far better to wait until the earth has dried out than to sow when it is cold and wet.

I cannot overstress the importance of fine tilth for successful sowing. The seed that lands on a clod has an underprivileged youth.

Anemone apennina makes a striking carpet of lavender blue daisy-like flowers. It should be planted in early March.

April
Week 1

Garden flowers

The sowing of annuals can begin if the weather is friendly. Work a general garden fertilizer into the bed or shallow trench prepared for row or edge sowing.

Annuals that can be sown safely providing the soil is friable include sweet alyssum, the morning glories, adonis, coreopsis, bachelor's buttons, stocks, poppies and mignonette.

When planting 'Heavenly Blue' morning glory, nick the hard coat of each seed with a knife or three-cornered file to hasten germination. A number of seeds benefit from over-night soaking before planting. Remember, morning glories prefer poor soil.

Spray delphinium, phlox and hollyhocks with a general fungicide such as benomyl as soon as shoots are 3–4 in. tall.

Divide clumps of delphinium as soon as growth starts.

Fertilize the perennial border with a good dressing of dried manure or Milorganite. Work it several inches into the soil where it will do the roots some good. Watch out for young growth that has still to make its appearance.

Check iris border activity with malathion dust or spray as soon as growth is 2–3 in. high. Repeat the treatment twice at ten-day intervals. Cygon® is another recommended control. Use strictly as directed.

Shrubs

The beginner should go round his rose beds a second time to make sure he has left no dead or crossing branches; the best of roses cannot be expected from old, hard wood. He must also make sure all newly planted bushes are firm in the ground.

A rose fertilizer should be given at the recommended rate.

Set new trees and shrubs at the depth they were planted in the nursery. Plant grafted ornamentals (but not dwarf fruits) with the graft union 1–2 in. below the surface (or at the surface in the warmer zones).

Virgin's bower (*Clematis paniculata*) should be limed, fed with Milorganite and, if lacking in vigor, cut down close to the ground. The new growth will flower this season.

Retie climbing shrubs. Cut out any wisteria that twines around roof gutters or grows under shingle edges.

Greenhouse

Basal cuttings of about 2 in. can be taken from summer-flowering begonias.

Don't allow the Indian azalea to go dry; if the plant threatens to burst its container, it should be repotted, using a peat and fibrous loam compost with a sprinkling of coarse sand. Being a lime-hater, the azalea prefers soft rainwater to a drink from the faucet.

House plants are best kept close in the greenhouse after repotting. Should the foliage flop, shade for a few days and syringe with tepid water.

Freesias, cyclamen and lachenalias should be dried off, gradually cutting down the water supply.

Lawn

Lawn care begins in earnest this month by brushing and raking when the weather permits. A roller should seldom be used and never when the lawn is wet.

The important thing is to fertilize before growth starts.

The new lawn, sown last fall, should not be cut until it is 3 in. high. Established turf should be cut at not less than 1½ in. and the clippings left where they fall, unless excessively heavy. An exception is bent grass turf: this grass should be cut to ¾ in. with a reel mower, daily when possible, and the clippings collected.

Vegetables

Gardeners in the north can plant out shallots, but potatoes should be risked only in warm gardens unless they can be given protection. Earlies only are worth the risk and trouble. Potatoes may be planted through slits made 1 ft. apart in black polyethylene sheeting laid on the ground. This not only discourages weeds, but keeps the soil moist and the temperature higher. The potato plants push through the sheeting as they grow.

Lettuce must be hardened off carefully; all the early sown seedlings benefit by spending a final few weeks in the cold frame.

When noonday temperatures average 45°F. (7°C.) sow spinach, parsnips, carrots and beets, and repeat in two weeks. If you haven't already done it, sow a few rows of beets 6–8 in. apart for greens and pull them when about 6 in. high.

Herbs

Chives can now be divided and replanted.

Camellia 'Furo-an', a single-flowered beauty hardy in sheltered gardens, but should be given protection until established.

April
Week 2

Garden flowers

Reduce summer grass-trimming time by installing corrugated aluminum grass-stoppers around border and bed edges. When these are sunk flush with the turf, no edging tools will be needed. Backing with a row of flush-set bricks will give added stability.

Mulch should be removed from gardens in southern zones. But do not disturb the mulch under such shallow-rooting shrubs as azaleas, rhododendrons, andromeda and laurel, or beneath conifers large or small. Add all removed mulch to the compost pile.

Small stone chips scattered close to and around such rosette alpines as saxifraga, lewisia and the dwarf *Armeria* will provide needed surface drainage and reduce basal crown-rot.

Ajugas belong in two places: *A. reptans* and its cultivars as superb ground covers for full sun; *A. pyramidalis*, nonspreading, as a neat, blue-flowered border perennial. Each is exceedingly hardy, and evergreen in mild climates. Plant as soon as the soil is ready.

Shrubs

Pachistima canbyi, of our Allegheny Mountains, is a delightful hardy dwarf evergreen shrub for rockery or border. It can be trimmed as a dwarf hedge. Left alone, it grows to 8 in. high and its trailing stems will spread to 2 ft. It will grow in any garden soil but has a preference for lime.

Greenhouse

It is time to plant the special bulbs to bloom next fall and winter. Among them Aztec lily (*Sprekelia*, red, this summer), Scarborough lily (*Vallota*, red, late autumn) and blood lily (*Haemanthus*, pink to red, autumn), Amazon lily (*Eucharis*, white, all winter) and clivias (orange-red, mid-winter).

Sow seeds of any outdoor annuals not already started: baby's breath, China asters, cosmos, coxcombs and salpiglossis.

Start the fancy-leaved caladiums for summer foliage. Tuberose 'The Pearl' planted now and set out in June will produce spikes of fragrant white flowers from late August until the frost. If you like the fairy lily (*Zephranthes*, available in a variety of colors), plant now for mid-summer bloom.

Hydrangeas showing new growth must be watered regularly and well. Feed every ten days with a liquid fertilizer. A small amount of alum added to the soil will encourage blue flowers. (See November, Week 2.)

Vegetables

Make the first sowing of peas in cold districts and go on sowing outdoors at intervals from now until June.

The gardener should get in the habit of sowing little and often, making the packet go a long way.

Tomato and pepper seedlings should be potted into 3 in. pots as soon as they are large enough to handle.

Rhubarb can be planted now. Use divisions from established plants of known value. I suggest you try the cultivars 'Crimson Cherry' or 'MacDonald'; you will find them superior to old garden forms.

Add Milorganite liberally to the soil before planting and feed with liquid fertilizer after two weeks. Rhubarb is a heavy feeder.

Following the onions and parsnips, sow peas, broad beans, lettuce and radishes in rich soil at intervals of 10–12 days.

Thin any outdoor vegetable seedlings before they become leggy through overcrowding.

Fruit

Where climatic changes are as diverse as ours, any spray schedule must take this into account. Here is a suggested program:

Blossom buds showing green: oil spray for sap-sucking insects.

Petal-fall stage, before calyx closes: malathion for codling moth, curculio and scab. Repeat with same spray in ten days, and again two weeks later.

Recently planted fruit trees should be kept free of grass and weeds at their base; they need all the nourishment and nitrogen they can get.

Recently planted raspberry canes should be reduced to 12–18 in., according to their vigor.

Primula polyanthus or primrose. Usually found in many colors in profuse clusters.

April
Week 3

Garden flowers

I am in favor of lifting a few forget-me-nots and potting them up for early flowering. They make good temporary house plants while in bloom.

A cultivar that deserves to be grown more widely (and is hardy through zone 6) is 'Royal Robe', a violet with very fragrant, deep violet-blue single flowers on 6 in. stems. It does well in full sun or partial shade and can be used for edging or as ground cover. It demands a well-decayed leaf mold and manure compost. The plants should be kept young, and crowns planted now are increased annually by means of runners. Unwanted runners should be dismissed. 'White Czar' is a large white-flowered counterpart on slightly shorter stems.

Gladiolus corms can be planted out as soon as the soil is friable. Make a cutting bed for them in full sun, and plant a row every ten days or so until mid-June. They will bloom in 90 days.

In addition to growing the usual giant sorts, try a dozen or two of the small-flowered, branching butterfly group (petals spreading, with blotched throat markings) or the conventionally shaped miniatures.

Of the butterflies, I like 'Haute Couture' and 'Segwin'; of the miniatures, the Dutch 'Atom' is tops and 'Candy' is also excellent. Although they have been on the market for 30 years, corms are rather expensive, so save the cormlets and propagate your own. If you have difficulty finding these, try White Flower Farm, Litchfield, Connecticut.

The hybrid *Dianthus allwoodii* has the merit of being a compact grower, is perpetual-flowering if kept picked and comes in a range of colors. Grow a few, then propagate by cuttings: choose the plant with the form and color you like best. Of the newcomers, Dianthus 'Magic Charms' is a top All-America selection.

If you have enough space—about 10 × 15 ft.—an aquatic planting should be considered: a shallow pool of irregular form (not necessarily of concrete), with aquatic or marsh plants on three sides, backed up by shrubbery. A $\frac{1}{2}$ in. water supply line with float-box valve and overflow pipe is a must. Such a planting can be both a challenge and a conversation piece.

Hardy waterlilies can be planted now. They are heavy feeders, so use plenty of rotted or dried cow manure. Hold back the tropicals until late May, when frost danger is past.

Spring bulb planting is the keen gardener's regular autumn chore, but more people should plant the summer-flowering bulbs in late April. May I remind you of the de Caen anemones, those single poppy-like flowers with black centers, and the richly colored St Brigids, the galtonias or summer hyacinths, the exotic tigridias in exciting colors, and others that deserve to be seen more often.

Shrubs

Still new to Western gardens but now available at better nurseries is the truly dwarf Korean lilac that grows only 5–6 ft. high, with very fragrant lavender-colored flowers. Buy a plant or two and propagate more by softwood cuttings (taken early). This plant makes a fine low hedge.

Where garden space is restricted, consider some of the dwarf coniferous evergreens that are now available in an increasingly wide variety of form, foliage color and texture. Be sure to fertilize them well, and use a thick mulch of shredded or chipped bark over perforated polyethylene.

When visiting nurseries, look for juneberry (*Amelanchier alnifolia*), a form of shadbush. The cultivar 'Alstaglow', developed in Canada, is exceedingly hardy and has brilliant red autumn foliage.

Greenhouse

Chrysanthemums, dahlias and bedding plants will now be moving on from the greenhouse to the frame to harden off. A fortunate exit, for the tomatoes will be hankering to take their place, demanding a temperature of 54°–59°F. (12°–15°C.). Decorative chrysanthemums should be repotted into $4\frac{1}{2}$ in. pots as soon as the 3 in. pots become full of roots; they can then be transferred to the frame.

Dahlia cuttings of 3–4 in. may be taken. If taken with a heel a 100 per cent strike may be expected, but no doubt there will be fewer cuttings.

The temperature may rise to 75°F. (24°C.), and the house should be ventilated early and closed up by 4 p.m. Water in the morning only; many plants not in flower will enjoy a syringe with tepid water.

Beware of a dry atmosphere in the greenhouse; it encourages red spider.

Lysichitum Americanum, an exciting spring-flowering waterside plant. It enjoys rich soil and moisture and is best suited for gardens of the Pacific North-west.

April
Week 4

Garden flowers

Crown-forming perennials produce larger and healthier flower stems when thinned. Snip off all but four or five of the strongest spring shoots when 3–4 in. high, particularly from new plants. Aster, baby's breath, balloon flower, delphinium, garden phlox, heliopsis and peony will all benefit from this attention.

Lily of the valley thrives in half shade, and enjoys woodsy soil, rich in humus. (It does particularly well under oak trees.) Plant with the pip tops even with the ground. To avoid unwanted spreading, restrict with corrugated aluminum edging guard set at least 8 in. into the ground.

If you find sunflowers to be too coarse a back-border plant, try the annual Mexican tithonia, in full sun. Sow it in a double row, thinning the plants later to 1 ft. apart. It will make a vermilion-flowered screen 6–8 ft. tall.

Shrubs

Replace any winter-killed roses if the soil is no longer muddy or sticky.

If the soil is not yet ready, heel shrubs from mail-order houses in a protected spot and plant in their permanent locations as soon as possible. Take care to plant them at the same depth as they were in the nursery.

Greenhouse

Plant up the hanging baskets with achimenes. It is the easiest of cool greenhouse plants and a splendid basket performer. Cultivars of wide color range are to be had. Place the tuberous roots $\frac{3}{4}$ in. deep and 1 in. apart in a good compost. Beware of overwatering in the early stages of growth.

Bulbs of auratum and speciosum lilies potted now will flower in November and December.

Softwood cuttings of pentas, bougainvillea and stephanotis can be taken as soon as day temperatures reach 60°F. ($15\frac{1}{2}$°C.). Old plants of astilbe should be divided and replanted.

Freesia bulbs, dried off after the foliage dies down, can be repotted for forcing again. Tulips, hyacinths and daffodils should go into the garden, and paper whites to the compost heap.

Annuals for outdoor planting, as well as coleus and lantana, should be pinched and fed regularly.

Lawn

The blossoming of mock-orange (*Philadelphus*) is a warning that crab grass, that annual lawn pest, is about to germinate. In anticipation, apply a pre-emergence control before those millions of seeds start germinating. Follow directions, and apply the product evenly.

I am often asked for my opinion of the camomile lawn. It requires less mowing than turf and is harder wearing: the close-growing plant seems to enjoy the trampling of feet. But I do not recommend it where winter averages fall below 0°F. (−18°C.).

Camomile seed should be sown in drills: the tufts transplant well and soon cover bare patches where seed has failed. Wiry stalks and unattractive flowers should be dismissed by hand or mower blade. It is, however, possible to obtain non-flowering plants which will quickly make a lawn.

Vegetables

Set out the kale crops (cabbages and the like). Spray them with malathion as soon as cabbage worms are spotted. In areas where the cabbage maggot is troublesome, either disinfect the garden soil with granular diazinon (Gardentox ®) before planting, or spray the plants with diazinon when the forsythia starts to bloom, repeating the treatment three times at ten-day intervals.

If you like Brussels sprouts, plant them in a rich loam that has been well fed. The soil should be trodden firm (loose soil results in blown sprouts). If there is not enough rain, watering may be necessary to maintain steady growth.

Fruit

More strawberries can be planted, but they must not be allowed to flower their first year.

A dressing of a 10-8-6 fertilizer, followed by a mulch of compost or of commercial chicken litter, will be welcomed by all bush fruits.

Summer mulches between rows of small fruits and asparagus are highly desirable. They retain soil moisture and reduce weeding. The choice of mulch depends on availability and cost; ground sugar cane or wood chips may be the cheapest.

Strips of perforated black plastic can be used in place of an organic mulch, but it offers no residual nourishment.

Narcissus poeticus 'Actaea', a snow-white, sweet-scented flower with a marigold 'eye' margined scarlet. An excellent garden plant that may also be forced in February.

May

The veteran gardener does not trust the month of May—it has treated him too treacherously in the past. But I love this month: it means lily of the valley and azaleas, followed by lilacs, and often a bonus of heavenly days.

Meanwhile the late May frost pays us out for any foolhardy planting. Plants, too, can be caught napping, having responded to a mild spell and hot sunshine.

Planting out from the greenhouse must be done with caution, particularly when the night sky is clear, and protection given to the impatient dahlia or over-eager potatoes and green beans.

Bulbs should be fed with a 6-8-7 fertilizer, or a prepared bulb food, before they flower or while still in bloom. Snip off dying narcissus blossoms. Do not cut or tie their foliage; next year's bulb and flower bud development depends on their growth now.

Two quarts of commercial garden fertilizer, such as 5-8-7 or 5-10-10, should be added per 100 sq.ft. when preparing a garden bed for planting.

Plants from mail-order suppliers should be plunged in a pail of tepid water. They are usually dried out on arrival.

Get busy in the herbaceous border, staking, supporting, pinching any leggy growth, thinning out the perennial asters and delphinium shoots, transplanting, weeding and sowing a few annuals to fill the gaps. Nasturtium is a sturdy gap-filler. Try the dwarf 'Crimson Jewel' or 'Primrose Jewel'.

Waterlilies and aquatics can be planted from mid-May through June. Make sure your pool is perfectly watertight before starting: a leak will be a constant anxiety. Waterlilies are easier to handle in baskets than when anchored to loam at the base of the pool. 'Sunrise' and 'Chromatella', both a sunny yellow with gold stamens, are hardy waterlilies not to be missed.

All bedding plants and seedlings under glass should be given as much air as possible. But beware of the late May frosts, particularly in the low-lying garden. Meanwhile, a sudden rise of temperature in the greenhouse is also a danger!

Earth up the potatoes and thin out the young crops in the vegetable garden, remembering that at this time of year Nature may do some thinning out for you.

Time should be found to mulch the fruit trees: they need nourishment and moisture at this stage.

Growing and sowing conditions are at their best just now and the garden a joy for it is lilac time.

Over the years the hybridizer has worked hard on the wishy-washy lilac, *Syringa vulgaris*, and has presented us with the beautiful double white 'Madame Lemoine' (1890), double violet-purple 'Charles Joly', the single soft yellow 'Primrose' and double pink 'Alice Eastwood'—each more beautiful than the other. Please do not leave out the Canadian hybrids, such as 'Esther Staley', single pure red, or 'Katherine Havemeyer', large double cobalt-lilac flushed mauve. The much later-flowering hybrid *Syringa prestoniae*, 'James MacFarlane', has desirable bright clear-pink trusses.

Spring-flowering shrubs that have bloomed, in particular the free-growing forsythia, can now be pruned; and any last planting of rhododendrons or azaleas should be made towards the end of the month, tucking the roots up in plenty of peat. But make sure the peat is thoroughly mixed with the soil.

This is also one of the busiest months in the vegetable garden. Don't make the mistake of leaving too many chores until the end of the month.

Add sweet pea brush before the vines begin to fall over. Select the strongest shoot of each plant and pinch out the laterals. String netting is a good support; summer heat makes wire netting unfriendly to sensitive tendrils.

Keep gravel walks and drives weed-free by the judicious use of herbicides applied on a winter's day.

A country garden in spring.

46

May
Week 1

Garden flowers

Choose a cloudy or showery day for planting out seedlings.

Lupin and delphinium shoots can be taken from the crown, dipped in rooting powder, inserted in pots of sandy compost and placed in the greenhouse. They do not require heat.

Annuals will germinate well when sown in the open.

Plants are growing fast now: stake and tie regularly, early rather than late.

Young growth of peonies will benefit from regular watering and three bi-monthly applications of liquid fertilizer. If lateral flower buds are pinched out when they appear, you will get handsome flowers.

Spray or dust hollyhocks against rust with any benomyl-containing fungicide (see under Week 3). Terrachlor is a second choice and can also be used to advantage as a drench for young delphinium growth.

Spray iris with Sevin ® to control borers.

Deadhead the pansies regularly. Shear off old flowers from arabis, anchusa, aubretia, cerastium and golden alyssum and a second crop will follow.

Shrubs

When evergreen planting is completed, try your hand at layering. Any free-growing rhododendron lends itself well to this task. Choose a pliable branch of last year's growth that will willingly bend to soil level; after making a slit on the underside of the branch, press the incision into a small heap of peaty loam that has been generously sprinkled with sand, and peg firmly with a stake.

I was taught the art of layering before I could read adequately, my father being a rhododendron enthusiast; at the time I found it a very dull game. However, I have grown to find it both fascinating and rewarding.

The layer should be kept slightly moist until it makes growth—a sign that it has taken root. Don't be impatient to separate the youngster from its parent.

Prune magnolias and flowering cherries sparingly after flowering. They do not respond well to severe trimming.

Lilac, deutzia and spiraea hedges should be trimmed after blooming. Cut some of the oldest stems back to 10–15 in. from the ground to promote new growth. Stout sucker growth should be pinched to induce branching.

This is the time to clip and train evergreens into shape, especially such hedge plantings as arbor-vitae, hemlock and yew. When too high, they will accept severe topping.

Spray birches for leaf miner when leaves are half grown or less. Use Meta-Systox ® or malathion. If the shrub is badly infested, repeat the spraying bi-monthly into July.

Plan to visit nurseries and public gardens while the spring shrubs are in flower. Keep a notebook and jot down the names of plants and cultivars to plant in the fall or next spring. If planted now, they must be container-grown or balled and burlaped plants. Beginners should select heathers when in flower in order to get just what they want. Some of the new cultivars of dogwood, forsythia, crape myrtle and broad-leaved evergreens should also be tried.

Greenhouse

I hope the schizanthus is now rewarding you for your care?

Sow cinerarias: they are a boon through the winter, flowering from December to April. The dwarf, large-flowered varieties, often zoned with white at the center, are outstanding.

Go on pricking out the seedlings of annuals before they compete for elbow room, and harden off the bedders for planting out.

More hardy plants that have been hardened off in a frame can be planted out, protecting them from slugs.

Shade the greenhouse with one of the special paints, or with slats topside which can be rolled up on cloudy days.

Carnations benched now under shade will give better fall and winter bloom than if summered outdoors. Be sure to feed them bi-monthly.

Vegetables

Thrill! The first asparagus may now be cut, but only from established beds that have been planted for two years.

Leeks planted early in the season should now be blanched by slipping brown paper tubes over them. These tubes must be fastened down to bamboo canes and tucked up with soil. This method is time-consuming; the less professional gardener will set his leeks lower when planting and leave it at that.

Spring cabbage will benefit by an application of nitrate of soda (2 oz. per yard run) applied in showery weather, keeping the foliage clear for fear of burning.

Prunus domestica, the almond, is hardy into zone 6.

May
Week 2

Garden flowers

All garden-flowering chrysanthemums should be planted out during a mild spell. Keep the rows at least 2 ft. apart, so that you can work comfortably among the plants.

Hardy and half-hardy seed can now be sown in the garden. I believe in sowing in generous drifts or, on occasion, broadcast, but sowing at stations will be found less confusing by beginners when weeding.

Sow the last of the annuals and then thin to 2 in. apart; those with tap roots, like the poppies, rarely transplant happily. Try the new prize-winning pure red cosmos 'Diablo'.

I have no sense of heresy in sowing a few annuals in the rock garden and a patch of bright blue *Phacelia campanulata* will enliven the scene when the spring alpines are over.

Marigold 'Showboat' has won more awards, worldwide, than any other annual. It grows to 1 ft. with double flowers 2½ in. across.

The seven-week stock, 'Trysomic', thrives in hot weather.

Shrubs

Go round the roses for the last time, with pruning shears in hand: perhaps you did not deal severely enough with the shy varieties. It is a mistake to leave weak growth on a bush.

Having completed pruning, the bushes should be fed with a ready-mixed rose fertilizer. If you wish to make your own, here is the formula:

10 parts potassium nitrate
12 parts superphosphate
 8 parts ammonium sulphate
 1 part iron sulphate
 2 parts magnesium sulphate (epsom salts)

Check rhododendron borer (which lays its eggs in May or June) with spray of Thiodan® or of lindane (where allowed). Repeat three times at ten-day intervals. Where these materials are forbidden, paint the bark of affected or suspect stems with a solution of paradichlorbenzene crystals in xylene.

Hedges

Inspect the lately planted hedge. Weed, hoe and remulch beneath the plants, and firm up the soil.

Greenhouse

Except in very cold districts, the more tender of the half-hardies, such as the morning glories and zinnias, can be planted outdoors. But be prepared to cap at night if a cold snap is forecast.

Sow *Primula obconica* for late winter bloom next year. Keep at 50°F. (10°C.) if possible until germinated.

Vegetables

Dwarf French beans can be sown in many gardens.

Thin the turnips drastically.

If you have pole peas instead of the more common bush varieties, support them with brush or netting when they have reached 6–9 in.

Sow radishes or lettuce between pea rows and in odd corners.

Cucurbits (melons, squash, cucumbers) can now be sown in all but the more northerly zones. Here is a rule of thumb: sow two weeks before the last frost is expected, but be prepared to cover at night if a late frost endangers or if planted in a low-lying frost pocket.

Plant six to ten seeds each in raised circular hills 10–12 in. across, the hills at least 4 ft. apart. Thin to three plants each. Four hills of any one kind will produce a wealth of vegetables! After the first true leaves appear, feed bi-monthly.

Sow zucchini squash in the middle zones, but wait until the end of the month in the northern. The F_1 All-America winner 'Aristocrat' is tops for quality and has a long fruiting season.

Herbs

Sow more parsley: there isn't a more useful herb.

Fruit

Reduce the number of young raspberry growths to that required for next year's fruiting canes.

Fertilize blueberries with an 8-10-10 or similar formula, mixing with it half as much again of ammonium sulphate. Apply two handfuls to each plant. Mulch heavily with sawdust, shavings or chicken litter and feed again in two weeks with liquid fertilizer.

Lawn

Clippings from lawns recently treated with selective weed sprays must not be used for mulching or compost.

Triumph tulip 'Carl M. Bellman', a mid-season group with large blooms on strong stiff stems.

May
Week 3

Garden flowers

A late planting of summer-flowering bulbs is possible in gardens well protected from autumn winds.

Biennials can be sown: Canterbury bells, foxgloves, forget-me-nots, honesty, sweet williams and wallflowers.

As the season advances you may have to deal with such fungus diseases as mildew or leaf spot. A new but proven product from du Pont is benomyl. A tablespoonful dissolved in 2 gallons of water will go a long way, and will also control red spider. Among other helpful preparations are MorGro Systemic, Sears Systemic and Alco Systemic. Follow the directions precisely. (Note that a spoonful is level, and no more.)

There is no hurry to plant out the bedding plants. If the weather is uncertain, it is quite in order to wait until the end of the month.

Dahlia roots should be planted out 3 ft. apart and covered with 4 in. of soil, but plants from cuttings must wait until June. If you want to plant out earlier than this, cloches or jam jars must be popped on at night. Dwarfs are best planted 16–18 in. apart for mass effect. All the tall varieties will require stakes 1½ in. square and 5–6 ft. long. Set the stake before planting.

Pick off pansy and viola deadheads, otherwise the plants will stop flowering and concentrate on reproducing themselves by seeding.

Waterlilies can be planted from now until mid-June. Warning: don't let them dry out while waiting to be planted. They do not require a great depth of water: 18 in. suits them quite well.

Pot-grown chrysanthemums, if hardened off, can be set out now. Add well-rotted manure or Milorganite to the soil beneath and around them. Pinch judiciously until mid-July.

Chrysanthemums are particularly subject to nematode infection from the soil. Propagation by crown division often spreads the infestation: it is wiser to propagate by cuttings from new spring growth. Set 3–4 in. cuttings in a sterile medium, and shade for the first few days.

Shrubs

Evergreens can still be planted.
Cut out all basal lilac suckers, at or just below the ground.

Repeat this treatment again if necessary.

Watch for oystershell scale on both willows and lilacs. Any shrub showing signs of the pest should be sprayed with malathion and the treatment repeated in two weeks. Heavy scale encrustations must be pruned out and destroyed.

Mugho pines should be sprayed with malathion for pine-leaf scale when pollen begins to fall. If lady bugs are about they may control the attack for you.

Rhododendrons or azaleas infected with lace bugs should be sprayed with malathion or diazinon (Gardentox®), especially on the lower sides of all foliage. Repeat in two weeks, and again in early July.

Sorry to dwell on pests, but it is their busy season.

We used to be told that this was the best time of year to plant clematis. But now that plants are to be had container-grown, they can be planted with little disturbance at almost any time during the growing season.

Greenhouse

Christmas cactus can be propagated by detaching two segments and inserting them in a sandy compost at the side of a pot. 'Christmas Joy', a splendid flame-colored hybrid recently introduced from Germany, has given a wonderful display on my office windowsill in spite of interference from the cleaner's duster.

Calceolarias can be sown now. They appreciate a cool place and a night temperature of 50°F. (10°C.). This comic plant with its brilliant pouches is not one of my favorites, but I must confess that the latest giant strains in yellow, orange and scarlet, "tigered" and spotted in contrasting colors, are very dashing.

Cyclamen can now go out to the cool, shaded frame.

Pot on the rooted geranium and fuchsia cuttings, and take more if wanted.

Wherever the frost hazard is past, plunge pots of cymbidiums outdoors in the shade or in half-morning sun. It is amazing how well they will reward you with early winter bloom if kept well watered.

Vegetables

Sow a row of your favorite sweet corn weekly from now until mid-July. Popcorn can also be sown now.

Fritillaria imperialis, the crown imperial from Persia, in colors from yellow to scarlet. Hardy with some protection into zone 5.

May
Week 4

Garden flowers

All bedding plants should now be in place (but in zone 4 and cold pockets in 5, wait another week). When planting edgings, have a care to keep the plants a reasonable distance from the turf and the rotary mower.

Sweet peas will now be growing by the inch daily: side shoots and tendrils must be pinched out and early flower buds too if you want good-sized blooms later on.

If the ground was well prepared, regular feeding will not be necessary, but the plants must not be allowed to dry out: a drink of liquid fertilizer followed by a mulch of well-rotted compost will not come amiss.

Cut back the lupin stems, and deadhead the pansies and violas.

Tulips and daffodils that are now faded can be lifted. Deadheads should be removed and the bulbs heeled in in the vegetable garden.

Make a final planting of pink, red and purple de Caen anemones, the brilliant St Brigids with their fluted petals, Mexican tigridias, montbretias, the exciting shell flowers, tuberoses and other summer-flowering bulbs. If you live in the warmer zones, add to your list the white star beauty, the acidanthera, with its intoxicating scent.

If dahlia roots have been kept fairly moist, they should now have developed small shoots and can be planted out in the northern zones, allowing 2 ft. 6 in. between all except poms. Place stakes in position first, please!

For dried winter bouquets, thinly sow strawflowers and everlastings, along with the globe amaranth and annual statice.

Fill and plant your window boxes, using a rich soil with plenty of potsherds around the drainage holes. Plant for gracefulness as well as for color by using some scandent vine-like plants (ivy and orange senecio) among the others.

Set out the cannas that were started inside weeks ago.

A few hills of ornamental gourds (grown on netting or stout twine) can provide an interesting vertical screen up to 10 ft. high as well as a supply of decorative fruit in the late fall.

Shrubs

Remove seed pods from the rhododendrons. In fact do not allow *any* spring-flowering shrub to waste its energy on seed production.

Make sure the newly planted wall shrubs do not go thirsty.

Cut out suckers from grafted lilacs and roses at their point of origin.

Disbud the hybrid teas.

Spray roses to control mildew, black spot and insects before diseases and pests establish themselves.

Complete heather pruning, using stout shears.

Mulch rhododendrons and azaleas with peat or leaf mold.

Roses: prune back any shoots that have not developed buds, and rub out inward-growing and unwanted buds.

Lawn clippings are useful for mulching in the shrubbery, but thick layers of over 2 in. produce too much heat and are dangerous. Reject any mowings that carry weedkiller residue.

Climbers

Feed the climbing roses generously with fertilizer and tie them in as they grow.

Greenhouse

Begonias and gloxinias sown at the beginning of the year will now call for 3–3½ in. pots.

Exacum affine is a pleasant small plant easily grown from seed indoors, and useful as a summer house plant.

Vegetables

Sow bush limas. I prefer double rows, each 1 ft. apart and the pair of rows 2½ ft. apart. Thin them to 8 in. apart, and side dress as soon as there are two pairs of true leaves.

Repeat the sowings for beet greens and harvest them when 6 in. high.

The last sowing for peas should be made now, but go ahead with weekly sowings of sweet corn.

Fruit

Maintain the spray schedule for pome and stone fruits (see April, Week 2).

Cut out any young raspberry canes that are crowding the center of the plant.

General

Conserve soil moisture and control weeds by mulching just about everything but the turf! Topdress each area with a lawn-type fertilizer before applying an organic mulch.

Wisteria, cheiranthus, bergenia (elephant's ears) and silver foliage.

June

June is usually coolish until mid-month, but the sun will be at its strongest. Temperatures will rise to 90°F. (32°C.) or more, but thunderstorms have the habit of cooling the evenings. Hailstones can be ruinous in many areas.

Roses are often said to be the epitome of June but their big display comes in July; honors are shared this month with the iris, followed by a galaxy of day lilies.

June is also the month for spiraea, beauty bush, butterfly weed, mountain laurel, hollyhock, American holly, coreopsis and yucca.

The chore of watering becomes ever more demanding and those who have not been able to mulch the newly planted will have to turn on the sprinklers once the sun has gone down.

Weeds too will grow apace but effective weedkillers do lighten the work of the modern gardener. It pays to keep the hoe moving.

Staking is essential: a sudden storm can play havoc in the border and ruin a whole year's endeavor. Avoid the stake that is too short, for when tied too low a top-heavy plant will snap off at the tie.

All herbaceous plants will be growing freely and will benefit from a side dressing of fertilizer, or a drink of it in liquid form.

The gardener anxious for first-class blooms will have to pay attention to disbudding roses and border carnations. This entails keeping the large terminal buds and dismissing all smaller competitors.

Evergreen hedges can be pruned lightly and kept neat and shapely.

Shade trees pruned now will heal their wounds faster than at any other time.

Softwood cuttings of spring- and June-flowering shrubs will root easily this month. Crop the leaves, shade for the first few days and syringe each morning.

Prune flowering quinces, lilacs, spiraeas, weigelas and viburnums as soon as they are past blossoming.

If an organic mulch was laid down last month, encourage bacterial decomposition with an application of any high-nitrogen fertilizer.

The rose-spraying program started early in May must go steadily ahead bi-weekly until October. Manet and Zeneb® are my choice of the sprays against black spot and rust, while weekly applications of benomyl are the best control we have against mildew. Avoid spraying when the temperature is at 85°F. (30°C.) or above.

Move house and greenhouse plants to a semi-shaded area of the garden. Plunge the pots, or set them deeply, in moisture-holding sand. Water regularly and feed every few weeks with liquid fertilizer.

The temperamental Jerusalem cherries should be kept well syringed with water when in bloom, and the young cyclamen and primulas potted on before they are starved and checked in growth. Watch out for and control the red spider.

Successional sowings in the vegetable garden should be "little and often". A semi-shady spot may be found for the majority of vegetables at this time of year, but the peas, vulnerable to mildew, must be kept in the open.

There is always some confusion among beginners as to when to spray apples against scab, so here is the drill: spray at cluster, pink bud, petal fall and fruitlet stage.

May I remind you again that sprays should not be used when flowers are in full bloom or the bees and insects that so helpfully pollinate the blossom will fall by the wayside.

As the days get hotter, water the lawn before it browns; there is less evaporation if done in the evening. Never sprinkle a lawn by hand; soak it well, *very* well, with a sprinkler.

A water garden in June.

June
Week 1

Garden flowers

Summer is in full swing: bedding plants should now be in position and tucked up with a little peat and fertilizer.

Herbaceous plants are growing fast and should be encouraged by light feeding. If slugs are troublesome, a metaldehyde bait should be put down.

Divide rock plants, saxifrages, aubretias and sedums.

Cuttings of pinks should be inserted in sandy soil.

Weedkillers should be used on paths when the air is still.

Iris fans should make a point of visiting specialist nurseries and growers for ordering now; mid-July is the best time to plant.

Many of the primula family, primrose, polyanthus, auricula, *P. denticulata* and 'Wanda' can be lifted and divided after flowering. The best strains should be marked when in flower for propagation later by division.

It is getting late to sow half-hardies outdoors, and an early autumn frost may cut their life short. However, you should get some welcome September bloom when those sown earlier are fading out. *Convolvulus major* always gives a good show.

Spray delphiniums and hollyhocks weekly for mildew and rust with any good fungicide.

Double portulacas love hot weather and full sun. Sow now wherever you need a low-grower and tree-flowerer, in shades of yellow to crimson. They will carry on into October if kept picked.

Gladiolus thrips may be controlled by weekly spraying with Cygon ® or Rogor ® , starting when leaves are 6 in. high.

Shrubs

Any shrubs grown from seed should be hardened off and plunged rim-deep in a bed of sandy gravel in a slightly shaded part of the garden.

Fuchsias appreciate acid soil and thrive on fish emulsions applied now. Water daily—they are great drinkers. Whenever humidity is low, syringe early in the day.

Boxwoods are highly susceptible to nematodes. Drench the soil with Nemagon® as directed on the label.

Locust leaf miners can be controlled with malathion now: they should be given a repeat spray during the month.

Now is the time to take softwood cuttings of many spring- and early summer-flowering shrubs (see December, Week 3).

Greenhouse

The final potting of all types of chrysanthemums for next fall and winter's bloom should be completed. Stems should be tied to canes, but allowance made for thickening. Exhibition varieties may require two canes.

Exhibitions, decoratives and singles can now go to their summer quarters outdoors, standing in rows on boards, slates or tiles. Should the plants flag, an evening overhead spray of water will lift their depression.

Have you given the perpetual carnations their final potting?

Cinerarias should be pricked out when large enough to handle.

Polyanthus can be sown for growing in pots: the seed is exceedingly small and should be covered with only a suspicion of finely sieved soil. At no stage must the seed and enveloping soil be allowed to dry out completely.

Seeds of cineraria and cyclamen should be sown by now in sterilized soil. Both germinate best when the night temperature is kept at 50°F. (10°C.). This may mean keeping the seed pans in a cool basement. Be patient. It will be 18 months before the cyclamen flower.

Senecio cuttings rooted now will bloom by Christmas. Shade and keep as cool as you can.

Vegetables

From now on head lettuce requires abundant water to shape up solidly. Bibb lettuce or the Chinese Cos lettuce are among the better hot-weather plants. All lettuces germinate poorly in hot weather.

Start feeding the tomatoes regularly once the bottom truss of fruit has set. A few leaves, but not too many, may be removed to let in the sunshine and hasten ripening.

Tomatoes benefit from mulching, which becomes essential if you do not stake them. Staked plants fruit earlier, but the unstaked fruit longer.

Dust broccoli when the dew is on with rotenone or malathion to check the imported cabbage worm which settles especially in the leaf axils and branch tips, where the flower buds arise. This little green worm has a passion for young inflorescences.

Fruit

Keep the strawberries mulched. Dress them with liquid fertilizer and water well in dry periods.

Japanese beetles are best controlled at this stage with the non-toxic Marcate® dust or spray. Sevin® should be used on ornamentals.

Clematis 'Bees' Jubilee', a free and vigorous-growing vine. It loves the sun and resents an acid soil.

June
Week 2

Garden flowers

Have you given the aubretia and rock cress a haircut with the shears, and the alyssum a light trim? The clippings will serve as cuttings; those from the new shoots strike best.

Gladiolus foliage should be sprayed or dusted against thrips, otherwise the pest will spread to buds and flowers. Cygon® or Rogor® are good.

Disbudding of roses and dahlias is best carried out with small snips, not fingertips.

Seed of selected herbaceous plants and alpines can be sown.

Winter-flowering pansies, and those to be set out in the fall for early spring bloom, should be sown in a well-prepared seedbed in the semi-shade. The soil must be broken down to a fine tilth; if the bed is not well prepared, it is wiser to sow in a seedbox.

Plant out polyanthus seedlings that have previously been pricked out into seed boxes.

If you use pyrethrum or rotenone sprays, discard last year's supply and buy fresh, for they lose potency sitting on the shelf over the winter.

Greenhouse

The Chimney Bellflower (*Campanula pyramidalis*), a splendid greenhouse plant growing to 4–5 ft., should be sown now for July flowering next year. It is also a good border perennial.

If more house plants are wanted, the decorative begonia rex, zonal and ivy-leafed geraniums, philodendron and cacti cuttings all strike well this month.

Shrubs

If not done earlier, carefully deadhead the seed-making heads of laurel and rhododendron, but take none of the leaves below, where next year's buds are now forming. Lilacs and tree peonies will benefit from the same treatment.

Keep a good mulch beneath the broad-leaved evergreens. They will repay you later if you feed them now with any azalea-type fertilizer.

The presence of yellowish foliage indicates iron deficiency in the soil. Correct this lack by feeding with a chelated high-nitrogen azalea fertilizer, or add chelated iron separately.

Climbers

Some clematis species can be grown from seed, notably the late-flowering yellow *C. tangutica*, the scarlet *C. texensis*, and the large-flowered Japanese *C. lanuginosa*. Each flowers on new growth and should be pruned hard in early spring.

Vegetables

Peas sown later than this week have little chance of maturing before the frost unless a fast-maturing cultivar is chosen. Peas resent dryness and should be given a rich moisture-holding compost, or be mulched well when 4–6 in. high.

Time flies and you have only a week or two in which to plant sweet corn. The new 'Early Xtra Sweet' matures in 71 days.

Endive and kale planted now will be ready to cut in September.

Spray asparagus with any strong contact poison (rotenone or malathion) to check both Japanese beetle and the smaller asparagus beetle.

Wilted runners on cucurbits indicate the presence of stem borers. They are difficult to control, and the best bet to induce new rooting is to place, or hoe, a few handfuls of soil over healthy stems at the leaf nodes.

Dust all cucurbits with rotenone or malathion to control both spotted and striped cucumber beetle.

Herbs

New growth of most annual herbs can be induced by pinching the tips. Keep sage blossom cut back in order to make more leaf growth.

Begin cutting and storing herbs for winter use.

Fruit

Cut out all unhealthy wood from fruit trees.

Plums and apples should not be allowed to overcrop. Thin out when weight begins to bend the branches substantially.

Mulch espaliered fruits and water them regularly.

June drop of apples starts now. Don't worry, it is a natural phenomenon.

A raised rock planting of lavender aubretia, yellow Alyssum saxatile, salmon-red and cream-colored rock roses and a bright yellow dwarf trailing genista.

June
Week 3

Garden flowers

There is little planting to be done now summer is here.

Deadheading is an important job this month, and needs to be given more care than it usually gets. Deadheads should not just be pulled off leaving ugly beheaded stems behind; small pruning snips do the job more cleanly and the stem should be cut back to a leaf or leaves.

Weeding takes time and it is important to hoe and get rid of the unwanted plants, for they take as much moisture and nutrition from the soil as the wanted. But don't stay put like a hairpin for the entire weekend; find other jobs to straighten you up!

Wallflowers should be sown this month for next spring's bloom. Late sowing is often responsible for poor spring displays. The seedbed should be given a sprinkling of lime and the seedlings transplanted after the appearance of the third leaf.

Baskets, window boxes and tubs dry out quickly and need daily attention. The basket will benefit by an occasional soak in a bucket or tank.

More hydrangea cuttings can be taken: well-ripened, unflowered shoots of about 3–4 in. taken below a joint will strike well. Crop the leaves, shade and syringe daily.

Another planting of gladiolus will extend the cutting season into late September: planting to blossoming usually takes 90 days.

Indoor plants

Be sure to water the Indian azalea and the Jerusalem cherry which you plunged in a shady place in the garden for the summer. Syringe the latter overhead from time to time.

Trees and shrubs

Spray birches for leaf miners if the earlier spray did not do the job. Use Meta-Systox® or malathion. Repeat the treatment in three weeks.

Roses cut in the evening keep better than when taken earlier in the day. Plunge the stems in water immediately.

Lawn

Keep the turf well watered and remember to soak thoroughly, and no half measures. Cut the grass to 2 in. : it withstands the heat far better than when shaved to an inch or less. In the south, keep Bermuda grass or dichondra to about $\frac{3}{4}$ in. high.

Where turf-browning is caused by cinch bugs, spray thoroughly with Sevin® (non-toxic to birds and animals). Should "fairy rings" or circular diseased areas show up, consult your local county turf specialist to name a suitable fungicide.

Moss or sorrel both indicate poor soil (soil that is too acid), inadequate drainage or too much shade. The moss or sorrel must be dug out, lime added (1 lb. to 25 sq. ft.) and the soil well fertilized. The bare patches can then be reseeded and kept watered.

Hedges

Hedges may be trimmed except the beech, hornbeam and yew, which must wait until the fall draws nearer.

Greenhouse

Hollyhocks, columbines, lupins, campanulas and delphiniums can be sown, and sow a packet of physalis, the Chinese lantern plant, for winter decoration.

Take cuttings of succulents: echeverias and crassulas strike willingly.

When the hydrangeas have finished flowering they can be repotted and, once re-established, plunged in the garden.

Chrysanthemums that have made growth since being stopped will appreciate a feed with a lightly forked-in fertilizer.

Water generously in hot weather, but beware of waterlogging.

Sow most perennials now for fall planting. But remember, many of the fancy-named cultivars may not come true from seed. They must be propagated, preferably by cuttings.

Calla lilies, both white and yellow, require a summer rest period, and watering should be eased off; next week, lay pots or tubs on their sides in a shaded place. They should be started into growth again in mid-September.

Vegetables

Asparagus-cutting must stop by June 21st and the plants given the opportunity of building up their crowns for next year. (Two-year-old plants should not be cut after the end of May.)

The fern-like growth that develops must be left until it dies in the fall, when it can be cut down to ground level.

Red and pink climbing roses on a brick wall

June
Week 4

Garden flowers

Go ahead removing deadheads, side shoots and tendrils from the sweet peas: should a plant yellow or discolor, it should be lifted and burnt. Sweet peas often suffer from bud-dropping. This could be due to overfeeding, but usually results from changeable weather or hot days and cooler nights. Do not worry; the plant will right itself.

Cut back delphiniums and lupins after flowering.

Iris can be divided and replanted, but wait another couple of weeks in northern zones. The rhizomes must be left showing above soil level so that they can be baked by the sun (for Japanese iris, see August, Week 2). The foliage should be shortened to prevent root rot.

The bed should be well drained: lime, bonemeal and superphosphate are all welcome, but farmyard manure may lead to rot. Firm planting is essential.

Add fresh water to the pool to keep the water well oxygenated. Beware of using insecticides against aphis, if fish are entertained.

Shrubs

Cytisus or brooms benefit if cut back immediately after flowering, removing leggy growth and any seed pods; exuberant young growth low down on the plant may be trimmed lightly. Severe pruning, cutting back into very hard wood, must be avoided.

Although not hardy in most of zone 5, cytisus does well in warmer zones and most coastal areas. *C. praecox* 'Luteus' has golden-yellow flowers and grows 5–6 ft. high, while *C. procumbens* with strong yellow flowers has a low-spreading habit of growth.

Greenhouse

Poinsettia cuttings should be taken from the best of the new dwarf cultivars, keeping a heel attached and afterwards dipping it in sand to prevent bleeding. The wound should then be treated with Rootone, a hormone rooting powder, and the cutting inserted in a compost of peat and sand. A temperature of 63°F. (17°C.) should be maintained and shading provided from the hot sun.

Pick out the best of the coleus seedlings, and discard the uninteresting. Propagate by cuttings.

Pelargonium cuttings can be taken, and cyclamen potted on.

May I recommend a greenhouse and summer bedding plant, the plumbago (*Ceratostigma larpentae*), to those who have not yet made its acquaintance? It is an enchanting woody plant with brilliant blue flowers freely given from August through September, and has every attribute but scent.

Plumbago is tender but can be planted safely close to foundations or with winter protection in the border in zone 6, and is hardy further south. Propagate from softwood cuttings. Keep a few in 8 in. pots for indoor winter bloom, using well-drained soil.

Vegetables

Tie in the tomatoes every week; the tie should be firm to the stake but loose around the plant's stem to allow for swelling. Remove the side shoots as you tie.

Feed the plants with liquid fertilizer every other week until August. The regular use of a fruit-setting hormone spray on open flowers is recommended.

Keep an eye open now and next month for the cabbage white butterfly. She will be laying her eggs now, and again later in the year. Eggs and clusters of young caterpillars should be spotted and picked off. Alternatively, spray or dust with rotenone.

Herbs

Many herbs are ready for harvesting. Chives, mint and parsley, and a number of the soft-leaved subjects, will keep well in the deep freeze.

Fruit

Raspberries waste their energy in making a surplus of new growth at their bases. Put on your gardening gloves and remove the growth just below the surface of the soil.

Mildew is often difficult to spray and control on large apple trees in small gardens; pick off and burn any affected shoots from young trees, and spray when possible.

Lawn

Reduce weed-spreading by spot control of clumps or isolated plants, using 2-4-D or 2-4-5-T in aerosol or squeeze cans. Avoid, when possible, the use of a general lawn-weed spray this late in the season, and never during a drought.

Escholtzias, the California poppy, available in cultivars of brilliant single to double flowers in dazzling shades of red, pink, orange, yellow and white.

July

Close hot nights and dry weather are to be expected in July throughout the United States, except at high elevations or close to the coast where evenings may be cooler. Lotus will flower in the pool early in the month, and rose of Sharon in the border late in the month in the middle region, earlier in the south than the north.

Keep your evergreen hedge nicely trimmed. Should you fancy trying your hand at topiary, clip a couple of yews in pyramid or corkscrew designs to stand in tubs at either side of a door. Topiary is a slow and ticklish job, but a fascinating pastime.

Meanwhile, the flower garden should in theory be a riot of color. You may not catch up with your summer border dream but if you haven't some color in your garden at this time of year, then your fingers are not green.

Deadheading must be done daily, otherwise plants will lose their interest in flowering and put all their energy into seeding.

The anxiety to seed is particularly evident in the short-lived annual that dreads departure without progeny. So don't let the annuals catch you napping.

When collecting ripe seed for home sowing choose the best plant of the variety for seed-bearing and store the seed in an airtight container with a screw-on lid.

The seed will not come true, the bee, not the gardener, having distributed the pollen, but seed-raising will be found a great experience. The youngsters are usually inferior to their parents, but there is always the chance you may be presented with an exciting new cultivar.

Plants are still making rapid growth and will benefit by a feed of liquid fertilizer; established roses will relish a pick-me-up after their first flush.

Foliar feed the broad-leaved evergreens, should their foliage turn yellowish, spraying the plants with a liquid fertilizer, such as Ra-Pid-Gro. Do the same for deciduous shrubs that may have suffered cold damage last winter. Foliar feeding with a fine particle spray assures faster absorption of food via the leaves than through the soil.

Sow hollyhock seed for next year's bloom. 'Summer Carnival', a carnation-like double, is an All-America winner. Destroy diseased foliage, spray the plants with benomyl and carefully cover the undersides of the foliage.

Pans of delphinium seed sown now should be kept in a cool cellar until germination has taken place. Then remove the pans to the greenhouse and keep them shaded. Syringe early in the day.

Gladioli welcome a mist spray during hot afternoons, especially when coming into bud. A mist spray started in mid-afternoon should be continued until an hour before sundown.

Geraniums and other spring cuttings that are now well rooted should be moved on to 6 in. pots before they become cramped and pot-bound.

The beginner must beware of a dry greenhouse atmosphere, otherwise thrips and red spider will be quick to take over.

Vegetable seedlings must be thinned; any further planting out should be done in dull weather and the plants must be watered daily until they are established.

Keep the tomatoes happy with liquid fertilizer.

Cut the cucumbers early rather than late, otherwise they may stop cropping.

It pays to spray potatoes with Ferbam ® at the beginning of the month.

The ground can now be used for early maturing carrots, beets, turnips and lettuce.

Thin out young growth of espaliered fruit trees, especially peaches and nectarines.

Perennial borders in a cottage garden.

July
Week 1

Garden flowers

Now come more roses, phloxes, campanulas, heleniums, hemerocallis (day lilies) and gladioli. Indeed, there are enough flowers for everybody.

There are few bulbs that can compete with the autumn crocus's bright performance given during the last months of the year. Colchicums, a close second, need more room than the autumn crocus. They are best ordered this month for planting in September; nurserymen seldom hold large stocks and the gardener who leaves his order until September may be disappointed.

The bulbs should be planted 3 in. deep where they can be left to increase undisturbed, maybe hidden by pleasing ground cover.

The jewel-like flowers, white and in all shades from blue to violet, with brilliant stigmata, are extremely elegant.

Asters, nemesias, marigolds and quick-maturing annuals can be sown to fill gaps where bedding plants have failed or are in short supply. Marigolds are a blessing for new gardens and small budgets: mixed with cornflowers or larkspurs they make a tremendous splash. 'Showboat' is a prize-winning double and sometimes difficult to come by, while 'Naughty Marietta' is one of the best singles.

If more rock plants are needed, rooted pieces of saxifrages, sedums, sempervivums and some of the other rock plants can be detached from over-large plants and replanted.

Indoor plants

Cuttings of aphelandra, cactus, coleus, ficus, fuchsia, plumbago and many other greenhouse or indoor plants strike willingly this month.

Syringe the Jerusalem cherry and ornamental peppers to ensure a good set. Spray the flowers with Blossom Set, a fruit-setting hormone used on tomatoes.

Begonias in hanging baskets and boxes need a good dose of liquid fertilizer about now.

Shrubs and trees

Prune back summer-flowering shrubs now outgrowing their allotted places, removing any old and unwanted branches.

Caryopteris 'Blue Mist', a cultivar of *C. incana*, is one of the best of the genus and hardy in zone 6. It should be propagated now from cuttings. It and *Vilex macrophylla* are prized for their blue flowers in mid- to late summer.

In hot weather, roses require the equivalent of 1 in. of water every week, given preferably in one, or at most two, thorough soakings.

Now is a good time to have eye bolts and connecting cables put into those trees with weak or very heavy forks, and often aged, far-spreading limbs. Done professionally the work is costly, but may well preserve a valued specimen tree from damage by high winds or winter ice.

Greenhouse

All free- and fast-growing plants will call for a succoring drink of liquid fertilizer.

Antirrhinums have proved themselves to be excellent pot plants, and the F_1 'Tetra' hybrids should be sown. The sweet-scented ten-week stocks are also a must.

Lilac, pink and purple *Primula obconica* is a desirable plant, but not for the gardener who suffers from sensitive skin or any form of dermatitis.

Vegetables

The importance of harvesting crops as soon as they mature cannot be overstressed; picking young keeps the plant cropping.

Feed the greedy onion (once a week, if you can) and hoe in the fertilizer.

Spray the potatoes with Ferbam® as a defense against blight, making sure that the undersides of the leaves are not missed out.

An early July sowing of French green beans may be the last of the season (depending on the weather).

Fruit

Strawberries that have now given three annual crops should be scrapped. When buying afresh, make sure of getting certified virus-free stock. Any plant now showing discoloration of foliage or distortion should be lifted and burnt. Unwanted runners should be removed from strawberry plants throughout the summer.

Protect blueberries from birds by using netting. Cover developing bunches of grapes with paper or polyethylene bags, and fasten with a stapler.

Rose 'Chicago Peace', a beautiful hybrid tea rose.

July
Week 2

Garden flowers

Sow English daisy seed (*Bellis perennis*) for next spring's bloom. Set out the plants later in outdoor beds in southern and middle zones, but in cold frames in northern zones.

Shear 6 in. from the tops of bachelor's button plants to induce new flowering growth, and feed well with liquid fertilizer.

Disbud laterals from some of the hardy mums to encourage larger flowers, and feed them all with a side dressing of garden or liquid fertilizer.

Among annuals to be sown now for autumn flowering, September through October, in all but the colder zones, are lupins, baby's breath, mignonette and Shirley poppies (*P. rhoeas*). Sow them where they are to flower; lupins and poppies seldom transplant well.

Propagate the tall *Campanula pyramidalis* and Oriental poppies from root cuttings. Plant pieces about 2 in. long and $1\frac{1}{2}$–2 in. deep, setting them out where you want them to flower.

Sow columbine seed (*Aquilegia*) hybrids for next season's bloom. Most of the newer cultivars are so superior to garden stock that it is a pity to sow old types. Allow them three to four weeks to germinate and prick off after the first pair of true leaves are $\frac{1}{2}$ in. across. They should be set out in the border in early October.

The best way to keep gladiolus stalks strong and straight is to set the corms a couple of inches apart, in a close-set double row, and to run string lines 15–18 in. from the ground on each side, fastened to stakes set at 3–4 ft. intervals. Exhibition spikes must be supported individually and firmly.

Stake any perennials that are showing signs of bending or toppling.

Shrubs

Have a care when picking roses: when possible make picking something of a pruning operation, cutting with discretion to an outward pointing growth.

Prune wisteria hard. Flower trusses will appear on next year's new growth. Plants reluctant to blossom sometimes respond to root-pruning.

Spray evergreens for red spider (they thrive in hot dry spells). Use Meta-Systox® or any good miticide. Hosing down with enough pressure to break up the webs is helpful but is no substitute for an insecticide.

Greenhouse

The 'Martha Washington' pelargoniums should be cut back after flowering. Plants from spring cuttings will benefit if the pots are plunged in the garden in a sunny spot, with each pot stood on a generous handful of sand. Pelargoniums must be brought back to the greenhouse before there is any danger of frost.

Perpetual carnations should be allowed to grow fancy-free.

Pinch back the December-flowering chrysanthemums for the last time.

Lilies in pots will demand top-dressing.

Do not allow the coleus to come into flower: the bloom is insignificant and the plant's energy better conserved for the ornamental foliage.

Sow Kalenchoe seed now for February bloom.

Cymbidiums and other pot subjects should be fed with liquid fertilizer and plunged outdoors in the shade. Nerine and haemanthus (blood lily) bulbs can be planted now.

Disbud the gardenias for maximum flowering next winter.

Jerusalem cherries and peppers need to be fed once a month until the fruits show color.

Vegetables

Leeks can still be planted, dropping them into 5 in. holes made with a dibble.

In southern zones plant winter greens, if you have not already done so.

Set out late cabbage and cauliflower, afterwards firming the soil well and giving the plants a boost with liquid fertilizer.

Chinese cabbage, a good hot-weather substitute for lettuce, may still be sown.

Sow after a hard shower in the hope that fewer seeds will be washed away by rain.

Fruit

Everbearing strawberries, pinched back until now, may be allowed to fruit on through the summer. Watering will improve both the quality of the fruit and yield. Feed now, and again in three weeks. Liquid fertilizer gets the quickest response.

Grass clippings that are free from lawn-weed seed heads make a good mulch for the small fruit garden. Spread them thinly to avoid overheating, or use matting.

Delphinium in a gay border.

July
Week 3

Garden flowers

When feeding dahlias, keep the fertilizer away from the top, roots and stems: some gardeners like to top dress the plants lightly with lawn mowings to keep the moisture in the soil.

Layer border carnations as soon as suitable growths appear.

Bedding plants are growing fast and will require feeding.

Canterbury bells must be deadheaded or they will stop flowering.

Geraniums and fuchsias should be well fed, remembering that standards have far to travel and therefore need a rich diet.

The last of the bearded iris must now be planted (see June, Week 4).

The compost pile must be turned over once this month to aerate the material and to work in recently added organic matter. When the latter is abundant, sprinkle with any compost additive, available at all shops, to promote bacterial action.

Add a dressing of dried sheep manure to window boxes and plants in tubs, and work it into the soil crust. Water regularly. If the plants are likely to be unattended for a week or two, mulch or work vermiculite into the upper soil to increase water retention.

Chinese lantern plants (*Physalis alkekengi*) are a favorite of the striped cucumber beetle. Dust or spray with rotenone or malathion, especially on the undersides of the foliage.

Shrubs

Grafted lilacs, roses and Japanese cherries must not be allowed to sucker (the suckers come from the rootstock below the graft).

Climbers

Cut back creepers on the house.

The passion flower can be propagated by young shoots inserted in sandy soil in a cold frame during the summer. It can also be grown from seed.

The fascinating blue-flowered passiflora, *P. caerulea*, accompanied by palmate leaves, demands well-drained soil and thrives against a warm wall. It is best bought pot-grown.

Passion flowers are very subject to nematode infection. Drench the soil with Nemagon two to three times during the warm months.

P. coccinea, a scarlet beauty reintroduced a few years ago in Louisiana, has become increasingly popular; it can be carried over in the greenhouse to spend the summer plunged in the garden.

Rambler roses should have this season's flowering shoots cut back to the ground once the blooms have faded, afterwards tying in young growths to take their place for next year's bloom. The undertaking is simplified by untying the stems, laying them flat on the ground and pruning there.

Hedges

Sturdy, almost impenetrable, deciduous hedges can be grown from beech, alder, hawthorn, hornbeam or buckthorn (*Rhamnus*). When kept trimmed at 3–5 ft. they are very attractive. Lining-out stock 1½–2 ft. high should be spaced 18 in. apart. Induce branching by pinching, and shape by clipping. Established hedges should be clipped annually about now.

In the warmer zones, holly, box and Japanese aucuba (available in several foliage variations) make better evergreen hedges than privet, barberry or camellia.

Greenhouse

Start feeding the chrysanthemums as soon as the final pots are filled with roots. Disbud the earlies and spray overhead with water at the end of hot days. Mulch the plants and water generously, applying nitrogenous feeds to prevent the stems from hardening.

Keep the chrysanthemums tied and limit them to one bud a stem.

Give the freesias plenty of light to keep them sturdy.

Vegetables

Bend over the top of the autumn-sown onions to check their growth. (The onions often do this for themselves.)

Sow fast-maturing onions for salads.

Early varieties of radish sown now and for the next three weeks will produce good crops before the arrival of frost.

Side dress vegetables about 2 in. from the plants with a balanced fertilizer, then rake it well into the soil.

Fruit

Young raspberry canes should be headed back with pruning shears to 2½ ft. and blackberry canes to 3 ft.

Peaches, pears and plums should be thinned to increase their size and quality and to sustain the vigor of the tree.

Calendula 'Orange King', one of the easiest annuals to grow.

July
Week 4

Garden flowers

Sow annual carnations in the border to overwinter and flower there next year.

At the height of summer the white, gray, gray-green and pale shades of color come into their own; gardeners who appreciate the cool look should make a note of the santolina, cineraria, maritima, white-green zinnia and light-as-air gypsophila, which are more restful to the eye than the hot sunset shades.

Plant crown imperial (*Fritillaria imperialis*) as soon as bulbs are to be had, covering them with 4 in. of soil. *Sternbergia lutea* is another bulb to be planted early and deep, in the hope that it will flower in the fall. Both these bulbs require full sun.

Shrubs

Heather can be trimmed back and mulched with peat. Cuttings inserted in sandy soil and placed in a cold frame facing north will root well in July and August.

Roses should be fed to encourage the last flush of bloom (but do not feed now in southern zones).

Cuttings of many shrubs can be taken at this time of year; side shoots taken with a small heel of hardwood from the branch should be inserted in a pot of good soil with a high sand content, and then placed in a shady spot.

Evergreens do not respond well to the knife (yews are the exception), and should only be cut back if trespassing on others or straggling; the majority are best trimmed in the spring.

The berries of fragrant *Daphne mezereum* should be picked and sown.

Climbers

Combined summer and winter pruning suits the wisteria. The young shoots should be pinched back now to five leaves and further shortened to about 2 in. in February.

Plants growing up trees, other than wisteria which is truly a strangler, can be allowed to go their own way.

Clematis can be propagated by pegging down shoots in pots of peaty compost. We are in the habit of training the clematis to climb but it is equally, if not more, beautiful if allowed to clamber on a trellis laid on the ground, when there is the added advantage of looking the flower in the face.

Greenhouse

The showy hippeastrum, better known as amaryllis, having given, I hope, its usual splendid performance, will now need a rest in a cool place, water being almost entirely withheld.

A successful octogenarian grower advised me to wait for the hippeastrum to break the pot before repotting, his way of saying, "Repot only when you have to."

Vegetables

Early potatoes, if needed, may be dug as soon as their tops die down, otherwise they can be left in the ground for another few weeks. It is usually better to leave them in the soil than store them in a damp cellar. Late potatoes may need an additional spray of Ferbam®.

Lima beans should be picked while on the young side. If the tip end feels spongy, the beans are usually ready to eat.

Sweet corn kept at 40°F. (5°C.) or at a lower temperature retains a sweetness that is rapidly lost at room temperature. This is the reason for home-grown corn excelling any bought at market or roadside stand. But prompt refrigeration is essential, and you must remember to remove the husks.

Garden beets may be sown now for late September harvesting. In middle zones another sowing may be made ten days later.

Cucurbits must be kept weed-free. Cover the runner's joints every 3 ft. or so to promote added root growth as protection against the vine borer. Additional feeding is essential for large yields of winter squash or pumpkin.

Fruit

Have all fallen fruitlets from the June drop been picked up and destroyed? This is especially important if the premature fall has been caused by codling moth.

Clean up the raspberry rows: old stumps are a happy hunting ground for pests and disease and should be cut down to ground level. Tie in young growth and treat the plants to a generous dressing of compost. Have a care with the hoe, for the raspberry has vulnerable surface-feeding roots.

Blackberries and loganberries can be increased by layering. This entails making a slit of 1½–2 in. on the underside of a stem, then bending the stem to the ground and burying the slit in a small mound of compost, pegging it securely in place.

Potentilla parviflora bears a succession of rich yellow flowers from mid-summer until the frost

August

August weather usually follows the pattern set in July. The atmospheric conditions are often similar and the two months add up to a fine or a very hot and sultry summer.

Although autumn has not yet shown any signs of taking over, plants and trees have lost their youth, and many are overgrown and blowsy.

If rainfall is low, regular watering will be called for, but the heavy dews will help to replace plant transpiration.

Many gardeners will be taking a vacation this month. Maybe there is a neighbor who can pick and enjoy your flowers and perishable fruit while you are away. If not, pick as many flowers as you can before you go, buds and all, to prevent seed pods from forming in your absence.

Root up as many dandelions and plaintains as possible before you leave; given half a chance, they multiply more generously than rabbits.

Ties and stakes should be examined. Don't leave your treasured plants at the mercy of a storm.

The roses should be given a last spray against aphis, black spot and mildew. If the earwigs are tormenting the dahlias, dust around the base of the plants with Sevin; you might also fill a straw-lined pot with water and float fish oil or fish meal on the surface. Many earwigs, lured by the bait, will drown!

Gardeners staying home will find plenty of jobs going begging. Get busy and blanch the cauliflower curds by bending one or two leaves over the flower or curd.

If time is available, this is an excellent month to sow a new lawn. Warm August soil is perfect for fast germination. See Week 3.

Now that the greenhouse is cleared of bedding plants, you have an excellent opportunity to paint and repair. If there are infestations of red spider, now is the time to eliminate them by fumigation or by spraying with Pentac.

Should August hang heavily on the gardener's hands, he might consider laying the foundation for a pool or rock garden. But he, too, has earned the right to lie back in a comfortable garden chair and reap the reward of his labor.

Meanwhile, the gardener on vacation has the opportunity of visiting horticultural and private gardens, nurseries and garden centers with notebook in hand.

I would suggest he look out for the lovely *Alstromeria ligtu* hybrids in pink, coral, yellow and buff that flower through July and early August. These are not easy customers, but thoroughly worth cosseting. The huge new hibiscus from Japan, 'Southern Belle', should not be difficult to track down, and the exciting new dwarf F_1 impatiens of the 'Imp' or 'Elfin' strains must not be missed.

Other plants worth finding are the dignified *Eremurus* or foxtail lily, and *Romneya coulteri*, the Matilija poppy, with gray-green foliage and petals of white, crinkled paper surrounding a golden center.

Search for the new ground covers and observe the conditions in which each seems to do best. New hostas are much grown, and some cotoneasters are fine when in full sun on poor sandy soils, which also suit the bearberry (*Arctostaphylus uva-ursi*).

Well-planted annual and perennial borders are always worth attention, for even if past their best they still have great beauty.

On coming home, you may find the old-fashioned roses in full bloom to greet you, and the white and mauve Japanese anemones may have taken charge, giving the garden a fresh look and some pleasant surprises.

How good it is to eat your own fresh vegetables again – cut younger, smaller and fresher by your hand than any other. And autumn strawberries waiting to be picked. A gardener's welcome and reward.

Kniphofia 'Springtime', hardy into zone 6 and known also as tritoma.

August
Week 1

Garden flowers

Many a gardener taking his vacation in August goes away with certain foreboding. Will there be a drought in his absence? To whom can he entrust his orchids and gesneriads, or the lilies that are the apple of his eye?

Take cuttings of geraniums, Martha Washington pelargoniums, double semperflorens begonias, penstemons and calceolarias.

Check the ties and stake the heavy-foliaged perennials in the border. Be careful to avoid bulb damage when staking the lilies.

Bulbs of the wayward Madonna lily should be planted now, in batches. Sit each bulb on a small cushion of sand. Sun is essential to this lily, one of the most sensitive to botrytis disease. Divide established clumps now, not in spring, and set the bulb tops 2 in. below the surface of the soil.

Hardy annuals can be sown in the border to overwinter; some of the finest larkspurs can be raised this way.

I always associate the nostalgic scent of white phlox with a hot night in August. This very charming flower shines out in the darkness, so make a note in your diary to plant the excellent 'White Admiral' for this purpose. Also plan to get a few plants of the truly dwarf (8–12 in.) 'Pinafore Pink' when autumn comes.

Divide Virginia bluebells (*Mertensia virginica*) while dormant. Mix bonemeal liberally in the soil around them. They naturalize beautifully along shaded streams if the soil is not too acid.

When cutting gladiolus spikes, spare as much foliage as you can; it contributes to the growth of the new corm and its surrounding cormlets. Cut spikes with a sharp blade (a razor blade fixed on the slant and given a handle is ideal).

Pyrethrum seed, best from commercial sources, will provide flowering plants for next spring if sown now in a shaded bed. They can be set out in their permanent positions six to eight weeks from now.

Select and order peonies for September planting. 'Scarlett O'Hara' is one of the desirable newer singles.

Indoor plants

Achimenes, which have given of their best, should be gradually dried off.

Shrubs

Go on propagating your favorite shrubs.

More hydrangea cuttings may be taken if required. They sell well at charity bazaars when in 4–6 in. pots.

Lavender cuttings, 4–6 in. long, can be struck outdoors this month. Remove the lowest leaves from the stems and insert the cuttings to a depth of two-thirds of their length. Plant them close to each other for protection.

Evergreens of any type may be moved when the tips of their branches have stopped growing. Here are three points to remember: water well for several days before digging; make the new hole large enough for the root ball and added compost material (beneath and all round); and fertilize with liquid fertilizer in two or three pails of water after planting (make an earth rim to retain the water).

Greenhouse

Pansy and fuchsia cuttings strike well in a frame, and can be propagated now.

Stalwart antirrhinums are to be had for next year by sowing now in a temperature of 59°F. (15°C.). Keep them in a cool cellar until they have germinated. Try some of the giants of the new 'Ruffled Tetra' strain.

Gardeners who prefer growing freesia corms to raising seed should plant six to eight corms to a 5 in. pot and cover them with $\frac{1}{2}$ in. of soil, afterwards placing the pots in a frame. The soil used should be nicely moist, making it unnecessary to water until the corms start growing.

Fruit

Have you cut out the unwanted raspberry and loganberry canes after fruiting?

Shorten the lush growth on the plums.

Espaliered trees that are looking dry should be given a thorough soaking, but peaches and nectarines now fruiting should be fed and watered with discretion.

Place a small piece of wood or sheet plastic behind peaches and nectarines growing against a wall to expose them to the sun; a few leaves may be removed if necessary.

Many of the strawberry runners can now be separated from the parent plant.

The hardy Nymphaea 'Escarboucle', one of the best reds after more than 50 years in the trade.

78

August
Week 2

Garden flowers

Autumn-flowering crocus and colchicums, ordered earlier, should be planted as soon as they arrive as they have a habit of rushing into flower.

If you have an orchard or wild garden where their lilac cups can spread themselves, a drift of colchicums (a size or two larger than the crocus and rather more showy) should be added. They are equally fine in the border, but their clumps of rather coarse foliage in spring are space-demanding and can overshadow colorful rarities.

Have you tried the everlasting flowers and ornamental grasses? They should be cut just before they reach their zenith, on a sunny day when the dew has dried.

Helichrysum should be picked before the central boss of the flower discloses itself, and heads and stems should be laid out on newspaper to dry. Neither stem nor foliage lends itself to drying, but the short-stalked heads are easily mounted on wires.

Dried flowers, with strong stems, should be hung head down in small bunches, so that the air can get to each bloom. They must be protected from direct sunshine.

Stachys olympica, (syn. *S. lanata*) or lamb's ears, respond quite well to drying and make a delightful surrounding to a Victorian posy of everlastings.

Keep your eye on the dahlias for sickly and mottled growth that denotes the presence of virus. Affected plants should be lifted and destroyed (burnt, if allowed).

Have you pricked out the June-sown wallflowers, forget-me-nots and polyantha primroses? They should soon be ready to move to the nursery bed. They can then be planted in their permanent positions in October.

Baskets, tubs and window boxes deserve a taste of a reputable pep-up fertilizer to keep them blooming until the frost. Work some Milorganite into the soil, and water it in with liquid fertilizer. Regular and thorough watering is a must.

Doronicum roots (leopard's bane) should be divided and planted now. Propagate by 2 in. root cuttings; this can also be done with the Oriental poppy. Add a few plants of *D. caucasicum* 'Magnificum', which have large yellow flowers that can be dried.

Iris can still be divided and replanted. Japanese iris require acid soil and lots of humus, and should be planted deeper than other garden iris. They do best where their feet are moist.

Phlox, sweet william and foxglove seed heads should be kept clipped. It is better to grow successors from fresh seed.

Shrubs

Be sure to step up the spraying of roses against black spot. It becomes more virulent from this month onwards.

Summer-flowering shrubs, among them the weigela and mock-orange, may be pruned after flowering.

Greenhouse

Prepared hyacinths for Christmas flowering should be ordered from a bulb specialist. They are likely to be a little more expensive, but they are worth every penny. They seldom fail.

A few pans of the heavily scented paper white narcissus and its yellow counterpart, 'Soleil d'Or', should also be planted early. Hold additional bulbs in a cool place for planting later.

Perhaps I should point out to the beginner that tulips are less reliable as pot plants than the hyacinth and daffodil. In any case, use pre-chilled bulbs of cultivars suitable for forcing.

'Beauty of Nice' stocks can be sown now and make delightful pot plants in the spring.

Vegetables

Keep peas and beans regularly watered and mulched.

Set a wood shingle under melons of any kind to reduce decay or wireworm damage.

Dust all cucurbits with rotenone to check aphids.

If the mature fruits of eggplants and peppers are picked early, younger ones will be encouraged to develop.

Lawn

A sprinkling of potassium nitrate dissolved in water is a splendid stimulant for a tired lawn. Use commercial grade, 1 oz. to the gallon.

Weeds should not be allowed to establish themselves, and a final selective weedkiller application may be given this month. If the weeds are scattered over the lawn, weedkiller should be applied to each root with an inch-wide brush fastened to a shortened hoe handle.

Magnolia grandiflora, an evergreen tree whose fragrant flowers will measure to 10 in. across. Hardy through zone 7.

August
Week 3

Garden flowers

The tall perennial asters (known in Britain as Michaelmas daisies), with their many new cultivars and increased color range, are an important group that keep the autumn garden gay. As the plants are particularly vulnerable to mildew in humid zones, they should be sprayed early in the season with benomyl before the powdery disease is established.

Have you disbudded the outdoor chrysanthemums?

Sever the stems of layered carnations, but wait to lift them until next month.

Take cuttings of violas and violets.

Forget-me-not seed sown now in beds will make an attractive display in early spring. Clumps can be lifted in March, or as soon as frost permits, for forcing indoors.

Cut hollyhocks to the ground as soon as flowering is over and burn all debris (where allowed). All seedlings that are to be saved should be sprayed with any reputable fungicide.

Order daffodils and other fall-planted bulbs, but control your impatience at their late arrival. The largest Dutch bulbs are the last to be dug in Holland and are late in reaching America.

Shrubs

Plants often droop from dryness at this time of year. A good soak must be given: dribs and drabs merely bring roots to the hot and dry surface soil which weakens the plants.

The benefits of mulching cannot be overstressed. It keeps the soil cooler and holds retained soil moisture to depths of a foot or more, reducing surface root growth.

Clippings from many evergreen shrubs will readily serve as cuttings. Root in a sand-vermiculite mixture, and shade.

Lavender can be trimmed after flowering.

Remove rose suckers.

Greenhouse

Heliotrope cuttings can now be taken.

Calla lilies may be stirred into growth after a summer rest.

Cyclamen should be brought in from the frame. Plants raised from seed sown now will bloom in 18 months.

Pot-bound cinerarias, calceolarias, primulas and others should be shifted into larger pots.

Lawn

When planning a new lawn, or the renovation of an old one, consider some of the newer turf grass cultivars bred for increased disease resistance, slower growth and ability to remain green in hot weather. They may be grown from seed. When not available from a local garden center, ask for them by name from any golf turf specialist.

Among the blue grasses, 'Nugget' (very hardy) and 'Arboretum' (drought and heat resistant) have superseded the Merion strains. They resent a highly acid soil.

Bent grass, best suited to coastal humid areas on acid soil, and 'Exeter' or 'Penncross' should be tried.

Perennial rye grass is greatly superior to the common adulterants in cheap lawn-seed mixtures, and 'Manhattan' and 'Pennlawn' are among the best.

When selecting a fescue for shaded areas, be sure it is one of the creeping strains.

Know the pH of the soil, and lime accordingly when preparing the area for seeding. One of the slow-release high-nitrogen ureaform fertilizers will give excellent results even though the initial cost is higher. Slopes to be seeded present erosion problems. Consider sprinkling with straw, more weed-free than hay, after seeding.

Vegetables

Lift onions grown from sets.

Dig up potatoes when skins are "set", and test them by lightly rubbing with the thumb.

Dust cucumbers weekly with rotenone to control aphids. If you pick the young cucumbers early you will extend the flowering and fruiting period of the plant.

Herbs

Cut down the mint and topdress the plant with peat and compost to encourage young growth.

Replant and earth up chives that are overcrowded.

A tight planting of Begonia semperflorens, Southbank hybrid, along with Cineraria maritima 'White Diamond'.

August
Week 4

Garden flowers

Last cuttings can be taken from the bedding geraniums. Plant them in some sheltered corner and treat them to a generous dollop of sharp sand.

Stake the tall perennial daisies that are now heavy with bloom, to support them against wind and rains.

I never tire of recommending the winter- and spring-flowering crocus species, which should be ordered now for planting in all but the colder zones. They are real jewels and far more precious than their large globular Dutch relations. 'Tomasinianus', with small flowers of silver lilac, and 'Gypsy Girl' of shining butter-gold (the petals are feathered chocolate-brown on the outside) are both good.

Trim back the violas and treat them to a tasty top dressing.

Peonies that haven't flowered for a season or two should be divided and replanted. Chances are they have sunk too deep and they must be lifted. Work a handful of 6-8-7 or similar fertilizer into the soil under and around each plant. If they are in good heart, leave them undisturbed, apart from an annual dose of bonemeal and a complete fertilizer.

Shrubs

Cuttings of many shrubs can still be taken by pulling away side shoots with a heel of old wood attached.

Try your hand at layering a magnolia or species clematis that has low-growing branches.

If the stems and underside of the foliage are marked with white dots, euonymus scale is likely to be present and a spray with dimethoate (Cygon® or Rogor®) should be given. This spray must only be used on plants listed on the manufacturer's label (not on mums or Burford holly).

Climbers

Tie in the rambler roses that have made new growth since pruning.

Greenhouse

The sweetest flower I know, and my favorite in the spring bulb parade, is the white Roman hyacinth. It should be ordered now as it sells fast and is seldom in abundant supply. Fresh and innocent, it flowers from November onwards, its far-reaching, ravishing scent leading us into thinking that spring is just around the corner.

Take fuchsia cuttings now to grow on through the winter.

When the gloxinias fade they should be gradually dried off and stored undisturbed in their pots at a temperature not lower than 50°F. (10°C.). The corms must be allowed to rest through the winter and may be awakened by watering in February.

Geraniums and 'Martha Washington' pelargonium cuttings, young heather shoots and shrub cuttings may also be inserted for rooting now.

Callas potted now will bloom in November. Set aside a few of the new tubers for planting next month.

Here are some bulbs that may be potted now for winter bloom; they require a night temperature of 50°F. (10°C.):

Lachenalias: water once after shallow planting, and place under bench for a month.

Freesias, ixias and lapeirousias: set a dozen in a 6 in. pot with bulb tips at soil level.

Dutch iris 'Wedgwood' and 'Yellow Queen': grow separately or mixed, four to six bulbs in an 8 in. pan. Set some pans in the cold frame to be brought in later.

Vegetables

Outdoor tomatoes can be hurried into ripening by being untied and laid on a straw bed.

Remulch the peas and beans and water regularly in times of drought to keep the plants cropping.

Go on earthing up and blanching the celery.

Fruit

Early maturing varieties of apples and pears are better picked before fully ripe.

To test for ripeness, lift and gently twist the fruit; when ready for picking, it will part from the spur.

General

Garden waste should be collected for sandwiching with layers of kitchen waste, grass mowings, wood ashes, etc. Thick caked layers should be avoided. You can hasten decomposition by adding a sprinkling of ammonium sulphate or one of the proprietary products to the heap.

Collerette dahlia 'Nonsense'.

September

The tall cultivars of New England asters and their relations, the Japanese anemones, are still giving a lavish display, but the annuals are on their way out and the days are visibly shortening.

The China asters do their best to hold attention, and the single daisy-like and button varieties have a certain charm.

October and November, the important planting months for southern zones, are approaching and trees, shrubs and plants must be ordered so that they can be planted while the soil is warm.

The gardener with a family and a wish to be remembered can do no better than plant a tree. Many gardeners must regret that their parents did not plant an oak, a linden or even a maple or magnolia to commemorate their birth.

Many of the service organizations, including local chapters of the Junior Chamber of Commerce, plant trees to revitalize shopping areas of the inner town and city. Through extensive breeding and selection, special street-tree forms have been developed of ginkgo (use the male tree only, please), Washington hawthorn (*Crataegus phaenopyrum*) and Lavelle hawthorn (*C. carrieri*), 'Shademaster' honey locust, mountain ash 'Scarlet King' and, most striking of all in autumn color, the 'Bradford Callery' pear. These same trees are equally well suited to home planting in urban areas where an upright, broadly pyramidal growth is desired.

For the warmer zones only, I recommend the aromatic rosemary to the friendly gardener who enjoys giving cuttings away. This romantic plant, with a host of sentimental connections, can be passed on to friends and lovers by a sprig (a half-ripened young shoot) in August or September. The rosemary is an accommodating plant that thrives in a light soil as far north as Richmond, Virginia.

One of the first plants to show autumn color is the woodbine (*Parthenocissus*) with its clusters of showy blue berries.

Other vines now in their glory are virgin's bower (*Clematis paniculata*) and fleecevine (*Polygonatum aubertii*).

Wisteria that failed to bloom this year should do so next year if root-pruned now. Using a long-bladed spade, cut a ring vertically about 3 ft. from the main stem. Then remove any turf within the vine and feed well with superphosphate. The plant should be pruned hard the following February or March.

Other significant work this month is the potting-up of pre-cooled bulbs in the home and greenhouse, and the planting late in the month of daffodils, snowdrops and other early-flowering bulbs in the beds and borders, or in the grass if there is a wild garden, adding perhaps a few of the brilliant tulip species that do not require autumn lifting and increase so well when left undisturbed.

Soil from the compost heap, with a dusting of bonemeal, suits the bulbs far better than manure.

Freesia (montbretia) bulbs can be planted as soon as available. Save a few to plant later. Keep the pots or pans in a cool place in a temperature of about 50°F. (10°C.), not necessarily in the dark.

The pre-cooled hyacinth bulbs and narcissus planted now in pots or pans should be kept in the dark for eight to ten weeks, at about 40°F. (5°C.). An easy way with bulbs is to bury them, pots and all, in a trench and to cover them with sand.

Cacti, other than the Christmas cactus, should be kept on the cool, dry side, but with adequate light. Water bi-monthly until March, then speed up their growth gradually.

Perennial asters, garden hybrids developed from Aster novae-angliae and A. novi-belgii. Better known in England as Michaelmas daisies.

September
Week 1

Garden flowers

The roses now burst into their second flush and the dahlias are heavy with bloom, while perennial autumn-flowering asters, hungry trespassers, take over the neglected go-as-you-please garden.

New England aster cultivars and their relations, overburdened with bloom, may need extra support.

Keep the dahlias flowering by removing deadheads.

Foxtail lily (*Eremurus*), in dwarf and giant forms, is to be had now in a number of yellow- and orange-flowered cultivars. When planting, select a spot protected from late March winds and avoid frost pockets. A well-drained but rich soil is what is wanted. Be prepared in zone 6 and northward to protect the plants when growth starts in the spring.

Rock garden plants moved now will be established before winter closes in.

Divide bleeding heart (*Dicentra spectabilis*), and replant in a soil fed with bonemeal and wood ashes.

Lily of the valley beds benefit from being reworked every three or four years. Dig out the bed, and fork in leaf mold or compost, with bonemeal or superphosphate, to a depth of 8–10 in. Plant only the strongest pips, just below the surface about 4 in. apart.

Trees and shrubs

Tree peonies should be ordered and planted now. They resent transplanting, so plant them in their permanent location. Prepare the soil to a depth of 10 in. by working in a cup of bonemeal and two of wood ashes to each plant. If on heavy clay soil, mix a quart or more of vermiculite when filling in beneath and around the plant; peat moss in any form should never be used. Mulch after planting.

Deciduous conifers, such as larch, metasequoia and bald cypress, should be moved in the fall soon after their foliage begins to yellow. They do best in acid soil, and appreciate an addition of peat moss in the soil beneath and around them.

Metasequoia and bald cypress are hardy well into zone 5, and both love to be near a pond or stream where their feet are wet in spring and summer. The latter is a slow starter but, in the right spot, is a rapid grower. They are very slow to leaf out in spring, so don't be in a hurry to write them off as winter-killed!

Trees with dead wood pruned out, and with weak crotches cabled, often survive hurricanes and tornadoes.

Greenhouse

Cyclamen must be brought from the frame into a cool, airy greenhouse before danger of frost.

Gloxinias and tuberous begonias should be examined regularly while drying off. Avoid dampness, and dust them with a fungicide.

Seedling gloxinias should be kept growing all winter, and not dried off.

Late chrysanthemums should be treated to a feed of liquid fertilizer once the buds have set.

Perpetual carnations and indoor chrysanthemums should now be safe in the greenhouse. The chrysanthemums should be sprayed against pest and mildew, using malathion for the former and benomyl for the latter. If infested with red spider, Pentac® may be useful.

Pot up a few colchicums and autumn crocus now for flowering indoors in three weeks. Hold back a few bulbs for later planting if a succession is desired.

Plants of schizanthus sown now will flower in March. They make good pot plants and the newer strains are splendid.

Have you tried any of the pendulous lachenalia in hanging baskets? Bulbs planted now, and kept near 50°F. (10°C.), will flower in late January.

Vegetables

Carrots are best lifted early; left in the ground they are apt to split.

Onions store well if roped and, where space is short, can then be hung under the eaves of a frost-proof shed. Start tying a large onion at the bottom of a strong cord, and then build up by tying on more onions until the cord is full.

Pumpkins and squash will keep better when picked thoroughly ripe. Do not pick them before the frost has killed the vines.

Herbs

Pot up a few plants of parsley and chives; store in a cold frame or cool lighted cellar until December, then place in a southern window or in the greenhouse for kitchen use.

Hydrangea macrophylla 'Blue Wave', the blue lace-cap hydrangea, with fertile flowers surrounded by large sterile blue bracteate flowers. A splendid ground cover shrub, hardy into zone 6.

September
Week 2

Garden flowers

Clean up the rock garden and the surprising debris that surrounds the ground-huggers, and topdress the plants with finely sieved leaf mold and grit.

When planting spring bulbs, do not forget the *Leucojum vernum*, the spring snowflake, with green-tipped petals. Left undisturbed, it will multiply.

Groom the pick of the hardy chrysanthemums and earlies before taking them into the greenhouse.

Short side shoots of perennials, previously cut down, may be detached and are easily rooted.

Don't allow untidiness to spoil the autumn garden.

Bulbs of summer-flowering *Lycoris squamigera* should not be planted too deep: 4 in. to bottom of bulb is enough. Mulch heavily the first winter, and plant in a protected spot if in zone 5.

Commence digging gladiolus corms when the foliage of each planting begins to yellow or turn brown. Ripen in the sun before removing tops, cleaning and storing (see October, Week 2).

If short of miniature or butterfly glads, save the cormlets and grow them on next season.

While northern zones may yet have several weeks of good garden weather, the occasional snap frost in early September can be disastrous to flowering annuals. A little protection on frosty nights may add weeks of colorful bloom in the border.

Trees and shrubs

Evergreens transplanted this month will put out root growth while the soil is frost-free. When planting, thoroughly mix peat moss and a cup of 6-8-7 fertilizer with the soil beneath and around the root ball.

Use liquid fertilizer as an immediate booster after planting each evergreen. Dilute as directed, but give each plant a quart of liquid for every 2 ft. of height. Then add a few inches of moisture-retaining mulch.

Climbers

Are the ramblers well tied in? Treat any wooden pillars or supports with Cuprinol. Of all wood preservatives it is the least likely to prove harmful to the plant and can be bought colorless as well as green.

Greenhouse

Has the shading been thoroughly removed from the glass? All available light will be needed from now on.

Pre-cooled bulbs should be planted without delay: they need eight to ten weeks plunged in the dark. Keep them at a temperature as near as possible to 50°F. (10°C.) to encourage root growth. Later bring them into the warmer, well-lit greenhouse.

Achimenes tubers should be drying off and the pots laid on their side.

A further planting of freesias may be made; they thrive in warmth, but resent forcing. No dark period is required. Bulbs brought inside from the frame in successive batches will give a prolonged performance.

Give the chrysanthemum cuttings plenty of ventilation and water in the morning only. Beware of uneven day and night temperatures; they can lead to damping-off.

The beginner knows that tender plants require varying temperatures. The following winter-time listing may be helpful when planning for later bloom. Ideal minimum daytime temperatures are given; keep 10°F. (−12°C.) cooler at night.

45°F. (7°C.):	chrysanthemums, heliotropes, schizanthus, pansies, violets
45°–50°F. (7°–10°C.):	anemones, begonias, bulbous iris, carnations, freesias, fuchsias, geraniums, ivies, lilies, plumbago, primulas, stocks
50°–55°F. (10°–13°C.):	calla, coleus, ornithogalum, nemesia, scabiosa
60°–75°F. (15°–24°C.):	gesneriads, orchids, poinsettia, strelitzia, most other topicals

Vegetables

Tomatoes should be picked and taken indoors to ripen before there is a severe frost.

Radishes sown in the cold frame will be ready to eat in November.

Swiss chard can be grown for another six or seven weeks if you have a portable cold frame, or wooden boards enclosed with polyethylene (cover the bottom edges with earth to reduce wind damage). Use narrow boards for best greens.

Fruit

Grease bands put on the fruit trees will trap the winter moths. The aim of every wingless female moth at this time of year is to creep up the tree from which she has fallen in order to lay her eggs. She is confident that the winged male will follow her.

Apples and pears ripen with exposure to the sun. Grapes ripen by the addition of sugar made in the leaves by photosynthesis, so it will not be necessary to expose grape clusters to the sun.

Cyclamen neapolitanum. Delightful miniatures with rosy flowers, hardy in zones 7 and 8.

September
Week 3

Garden flowers

The best of the hardy chrysanthemums intended for propagation later on should be labelled with tie-ons.

Border carnations, layered in July and now rooted, may be separated from the parent plant.

New beds or borders that are to be made should be dug now.

Transplant biennial seedlings to their permanent positions, among them candytuft, Canterbury bells (*Campanula medium*), delphiniums, dusty miller (*Lychnis coronaria*), foxgloves and sweet william.

The gardener who has not raised plants from seed can buy youngsters in flats or peat pots from garden centers.

Arabis, baskets of gold alyssum and creeping phlox can be set out now for early spring bloom.

Cannas in northern zones can be dug and dried off any time after the first killing frost (see October, Week 1, for storage).

Gourds grown for decoration should be picked before the first severe frost. Keep about 2 in. of stem attached to each fruit until dry (see October, Week 3).

Bulbous iris may be planted in the garden in zones 7 and 8, and with heavy mulch protection in zone 6.

Shrubs

When moving larger plants such as conifers and evergreens, reduce the shock by preparing for lifting. This can be done by driving a spade deep down around the plant, which will sever large roots and induce the plant to form fibrous roots.

Indoor plants

Those in northern zones will already have been brought in, and those in the middle and southern zones should also come inside now. Before moving, inspect them carefully for mealybug and red spider, spraying the enemy with Pentac ®. Don't bring a lousy plant into a clean house!

When the move is completed, wash off the soiled foliage and clean the pots.

Check cymbidium leaves for rust infection, and spray if necessary.

Pot up a few gay polyantha primulas and place them in a frame or greenhouse for early flowering.

In northern zones geraniums, fuchsias, begonias, heliotropes and tender subjects should now be in the greenhouse, and cyclamen and primulas brought in from the frame.

Geranium and fuchsia cuttings must be examined regularly for gray mold and any sufferer dismissed.

Outside chrysanthemums should be housed without delay.

Sweet peas under glass are something of a luxury. They should be sown in September (four seeds to a 5 in. pot). When potted on in January they can be plunged up to the rim in the greenhouse bench. Maintain a steady temperature of 63°F. (17°C.); a high temperature, even for an hour, might prove fatal.

Vegetables

This is harvest time: go ahead with the storing, clearing the ground as you go. Harvest the crops just before they reach their prime and do not allow the plants to put their energy into ripening seed.

Fruit

A new bed of strawberries may be made this month. Certified virus-free stock should be bought from a reputable source. Planting should be completed by the end of the month.

Pears should be picked when a little too firm to be eaten. Store for a week in a cool dark place, then bring them to the table. Late varieties should be stored for two weeks or more before using.

Lawn

Keep the mower handy, and avoid letting the grass go into the winter with toppling growth. There is a tendency to stop mowing too early in the season.

Bare patches can still be seeded. But pulverize the soil at least 2 in. deep and work in a lawn fertilizer before sowing. If it is a blue grass lawn, add an application of bonemeal or ground limestone.

Puff balls and fairy rings have a habit of appearing at this time of year. When brushed away, they may leave a tell-tale green circle and later a thin line of bare earth.

The ring should be deeply spiked with a tine fork and well soaked with a solution of 2 oz. of Epsom salts to the gallon.

If the fairy ring infection is severe, consult your local turf specialist for a more potent fungicide.

The gorgeous colorful vine, Convolvulus 'Royal Ensign'.

September
Week 4

Garden flowers

Label the dahlias carefully and decide which cultivars are worth propagating.

Thin the autumn-sown annuals before they get leggy.

The division of herbaceous plants can begin.

A batch of *Fritillaria meleagris*, snake's-head lily, planted in the rock garden now, is always an early spring attraction.

All bulbs of the narcissus group should be planted by this week if possible. Unfortunately the best of Dutch bulbs arrive at the distributors later than this. Gardens in the northern zones, where early planting is more essential, should try Oregon- or Michigan-grown bulbs.

Trees and shrubs

Deciduous shrubs in the southern zone transplant well in the fall, but there will be fewer failures in northern zones if you wait until spring when a long period of growth follows the traumatic exposure.

This applies to roses, and even more so to magnolias and tulip trees. Buy container-grown specimens of these two, for they resent root disturbance.

Lilacs moved now in zone 6 will transplant better than if moved after their buds have swelled in spring. Gardeners north of zone 6 should wait until spring to take action.

Hedges

Prepare for planting deciduous hedges: deep preparation of the soil is rewarding. A hedge of young beech trees set 18 in. apart is a pleasant change from common privet. Beeches respond splendidly to trimming and become almost impenetrable.

Greenhouse

Geraniums lifted from the garden should have their top growth cut back to half their length and their roots trimmed. They should be boxed and their roots covered with 2 in. of loam (or they can be potted up). They should be kept on the dry side through the winter.

Tropical gesneriads require a minimum night temperature of 57°F. (14°C.) and prefer 75°F. (24°C.) during the day. Partial shade is required throughout the winter. Here is a suitable soil for most tropicals: $\frac{1}{3}$ loam, $\frac{1}{3}$ sand or finely chopped osmunda fiber, and $\frac{1}{3}$ sphagnum or peat moss. Rainwater is ideal but not essential. A moderate to high humidity is a must.

Episcias, achimenes and columneas are all superb basket plants; African violets, streptocarpus and gloxinias are pot plants. They are fascinating subjects if you have the required heat, and are available in a wide variety of named cultivars.

Lachenalia bulb pans should be brought in from frames.

Vegetables

Cut asparagus to ground level when the foliage discolors, and clear the beds of weeds and debris.

Cabbage stumps should be cut up in sections and put on the compost heap, or you may dry and burn them.

When the same area is used each year, improve the soil by sowing winter rye now (broadcast, and raked into the soil). By freeze-up time it will be 4–5 in. high. When rototilled in the spring it will have reduced erosion by wind, and will add humus to the soil.

Parsley sown in the cold frame will keep the kitchen supplied through December if covered with a sash when regular frosts begin.

Fruit

Prune out old wood on peaches and nectarines.

After fruit-picking, old blackberry and loganberry canes should be cut down to ground level and the young growth tied in.

I am always surprised that more gardeners in the southern zones don't grow the delicious fig. If you live in a warm district and have a sheltered position going begging, I can recommend the slightly tender 'Brown Turkey', a good cropper if the roots are kept within bounds, with large yellow-green fruit of considerable sweetness.

Meanwhile, the townsman will find the fig a handsome foliage plant capable of hiding and decorating a grim wall, while requiring a minimum of root room.

The Pool

Give the fish a regular protein feed now that Nature's supplies are getting scarce. This will enable the fish to build up a store of nourishment before the winter, a useful larder when they cease to feed in cold weather.

Hibiscus rosa-sinensis. New cultivars hardy into zone 6 are now being released of hybrids developed at the U.S. National Arboretum in Washington, D.C.

October

This is the month when Jack Frost wields his paint brush across the wooded hills of the Alleghenies, the Adirondacks, the Ozarks and the New England states. It is the month when asters, birches, goldenrods, maples, oaks and milkweed pods dominate the landscape.

Plan to visit one or more of the leading arboreta or better public parks to admire the brilliance of autumn color and abundance of fruits.

In the garden, autumn crocuses are at their peak: *Crocus speciosus* in blue and white, *C. kotschyanus* (incorrectly sold as *C. zonatus*) with pale lilac bloom, later joined by *C. laevigatus* and the rose-colored *C. longiflorus*. Jot down names of cultivars that appeal to you, and add some of them next year.

October is clean-up month in the garden. Mix in your compost pile together with the annual leaf fall. Plastic-coated wire fence enclosures, about 4 ft. high, made for holding compost material are readily available. Mix in ammonium sulphate or a commercial compost compound as you build up the heap.

Work done this month will be the reward next spring!

In southern zones shrubs can be safely planted, but for northern gardens there is sense in waiting until spring.

Harden your heart and dismiss the summer bedding even if it is still giving a little color. The spring bedders—polyanthus, primroses, wallflowers and forget-me-nots—must be planted now and given time to settle in before winter comes.

Herbaceous subjects can be planted unless on heavy soil, in exposed districts or difficult town gardens, where it is wiser to wait until the spring.

More attention might be paid to the later-flowering hardy chrysanthemums that hold interest in the garden through October and into November.

Exhibitions of the newest hardy chrysanthemums are invariably given this month by horticulture departments at state universities, in many municipal parks and by some leading nurseries. No other outdoor perennial boasts so diverse a range of size, form and color. It is wiser to make selections for next year from the plants themselves than from descriptions given in catalogues.

Roses affected with black spot should continue to be sprayed until the foliage drops, using a fungicide such as Ferbam, Captan or Zineb. Spray downwind, the full length of the stems, and into the surrounding earth.

When is the best time to plant roses? Regardless of the zone, you will have to wait until dormant plants are available in the market. They should be planted early enough to spend at least two weeks in the ground before it freezes. Choosing the right planting date is always a gamble.

Tulips should be planted this month in all but the more southern zones. If not already ordered, see Week 4.

The greenhouse must be well ventilated during the day.

Shading should have been removed from the glass: the plants now need all the sun and light they can get.

Keep the greenhouse as clean as a hospital ward, free of bugs and fungi.

A propagation box—a flat box with the bottom removed, covered with glass—set on the bench, is needed for striking cuttings. Fill with a mixture of $2-2$ sterile sand and $\frac{1}{3}$ vermiculite.

Fruit ready for picking will part willingly from the joint. It may be necessary to pick over a tree several times.

Don't be in a hurry to retire the lawn mower. Set the blades for the highest cut and, where the ground remains free of frost, be ready to mow again next month.

Autumn foliage in Vermont.

October
Week 1

Garden flowers

The autumn overhaul of the herbaceous border now begins. Large clumps of the tall perennial asters and other trespassers should be lifted and divided.

The peony should be manured generously. The kniphofia and hemerocallis are best left undisturbed for a few seasons. Plan to divide them every four or five years.

The sooner the spring bedders and biennials, forget-me-nots and others are in place the better.

Polyantha may resent being planted in the same place every year so, if possible, find them a different situation this fall.

Pot up a few of the bedding fibrous begonias before they are killed by frost; they will flower in the greenhouse or on a sunny windowsill indoors, and serve as stock for cuttings.

Tender plants, such as heliotrope, plumbago and pelargonium, have now been lifted and placed under glass or brought indoors, except in southern zones. Be sure to move them before the frost strikes.

Summer bulbs are slightly tender and should be lifted from zone 6 northward, or covered with mulch before the danger of frost.

Begonia tubers must be lifted, boxed, dried off and stored. Bulb planting should be completed as soon as possible, except for tulips which can wait until November.

Put down a 10–12 in. label where spring bulbs, clusters of lilies and perennials have been planted. Only the exceptional gardener will recall all these spots come planting time next spring.

Also mark the places where the late-appearing perennials will take over, among them the aconite, balloon flower, Japanese anemone, mallow and perennial aster.

It is not too late to plant regal lily bulbs among the peonies. Set in holes 5–8 in. deep on a 1 in. cushion of sand, and cover with good soil.

Gladioli, from zone 6 southward, are best lifted this month and air-dried. Cut the foliage an inch above the corm. Later on discard the old ones. (See Week 2 for note on storage.) Cormlets, cleaned and labelled, should go in individual paper bags.

Cannas, especially the newer dwarfs, are difficult to over-winter, and some gardeners treat them as expendable. If kept, leave the soil around each bulb and store in boxes of compost in a cool dark cellar. In southern zones they should survive outdoors, if mulched, and also in zone 6 when inter-planted among the foundation evergreens.

Store Peruvian daffodil bulbs (*Ismene*) at temperatures of 60°F. (15°C.) or above for the first six weeks, and then at no less than 45°F. (7°C.) if they are to blossom the next season.

Shrubs

Evergreen planting should be completed before the middle of the month.

Hardwood cuttings can be taken from woody plants.

Rake all rose foliage from the ground and destroy it. It is probably diseased.

Greenhouse

If in the past year pests have been troublesome, the house should be fumigated with smoke pellets and given a thorough wash down with a Lysol solution to which a soap detergent has been added. Care must be taken to keep the solution away from all plants.

When frost threatens in the middle zones, the tender geraniums, fuchsias, chrysanthemums, plumbago, heliotrope, Indian azalea, solanum (Jerusalem cherry), and other plants that have been taking the air in the garden, should be hurried in.

Geraniums can be boxed, their roots covered with soil, or planted in pots for the winter. They must be kept in a frost-proof, well-ventilated place in a temperature that does not fall below 39°F. (4°C.). Pot plants are happier left in their containers. Regular watering is not necessary, but the geranium must not be allowed to become desert-dry.

Pot on cinerarias and stocks.

Christmas cacti, now available in a number of hybrids and cultivars, continue to need rest. Keep in a cool, darkish place and withhold water.

Meanwhile keep the potted citrus cool and rather parched for at least three more months.

Vegetables

Go ahead and clear all crops and dig vacant ground. Pea and bean vines can go on the compost heap.

Root crops (beets, carrots) should be dug before the ground freezes. Store them in boxes of sand kept slightly moist, at no more than 10°F. (−12°C.) above freezing.

Pompon chrysanthemum 'Little Dorrit' may be planted out in the garden in late May.

October
Week 2

Garden flowers

Here are a few notes for beginners on planting out spring bulbs. When interplanting polyanthus and forget-me-nots with bulbs, the bedders should go in first.

Plant spring bulbs and species tulips in clutches of a half dozen bulbs each.

Add a few groups of small bulbs to the rock garden, among them puschkinia, crocus species and muscari 'Blue Spike'. Wait another two weeks to plant new perennials.

Plant lily bulbs as soon as they arrive. Insert 10–12 in. labels before covering each bulb or cluster. Where soil is heavy, set each bulb on 1 in. of sand and work some compost around it.

When gladiolus corms are not numerous, store in stout paper bags, and control thrips with a light sprinkling of malathion dust before tying the tops. Keep in a dry cool place at 50°F. (10°C.). Small numbers can hang from nails in cellar beams; larger quantities are better placed in shallow trays or flats.

Shrubs

Early autumn is the time to give all deciduous shrubs a dressing of superphosphate. Work it into the soil. Bonemeal, however, is costly for the food value derived from it.

In southern zones camellia buds will be swelling and the sasanquas about to bloom. Feed them and don't let them suffer from lack of water.

Do the same for the roses, to encourage flowering in the fall.

Camellias are not strictly southern shrubs. Much has been done in recent years to produce cultivars of *C. japonica* that are hardy in milder parts of zone 6. They are 'Blood of China', 'Elegans', 'Jarvus Red', 'Mahotiana', 'Bernice Boddy' and 'Leucantha'. Among the sasanquas I recommend 'Maiden's Blush' and 'Susan'. Grow them as you would azaleas, remembering that it is the flower buds, not the foliage, that are the more sensitive to cold.

Greenhouse

Plant Dutch bulbs first for cold frame storage and later for greenhouse forcing and winter bloom. Gardeners without a cold frame should plunge their pots or pans level with the ground, and then cover with some sand, a foot of leaves, and boards or wire netting. Allow the containers to stay like this for nine to ten weeks in order to make good root growth at 40°F. (5°C.) before bringing them in. Most of the bulbs will bloom in two to three weeks given a daytime temperature of 60°F. (15°C.) (cooler at night).

Bulbous iris in pots or pans will be ready to cut in February if planted now and given a daytime temperature of 55°F. (13°C.). Keep them moderately watered but never allow them to dry out.

Delay forcing the tulips until mid-January.

The cineraria is temperamental and liable to collapse if allowed either to go over-dry or soggy, so have a care! Extremes of temperature must also be avoided.

Carnations should be staked with special circular wire supports and should be disbudded, leaving the central terminal bud on each stem.

Pot on schizanthus into the next-sized pots, when necessary. When they are allowed to become pot-bound, their growth and flowering are checked.

Hardy plants, among them the astilbes and Solomon's seal, can be potted up for early spring flowering in the greenhouse. *Dicentra spectabilis*, the bleeding heart, lends itself willingly to this move. A few pots of blue polyanthus plunged in a sheltered spot outdoors until January, and then brought into the greenhouse, will also be found most rewarding.

Vegetables

Where allowed, keep the bonfire going and burn up the debris that always harbors pest and disease. If a bonfire is taboo, put the refuse in plastic leaf bags with the rubbish. It should not be composted.

Pick unripened tomatoes now in southern zones and store in any reasonably dark place. Sunlight is not needed.

Lawn

Heavy leaf accumulation can smother the turf if not raked and removed periodically. For large areas, the renting of a lawn sweeper should be considered when most of the leaves have fallen.

Fruit

All dead, weak and crossing branches should be cut out from tree and bush fruits. Wounds of over 1 in. should be painted with a protective paint.

Rake and destroy diseased leaves and wormy fruits under the trees.

Romneya coulteri, the California tree poppy, flowering in late summer. It requires a sheltered spot and winter protection in zone 6.

October
Week 3

Garden flowers

The pick of the hardy chrysanthemums should be cut down, lifted and placed in a frame. The clumps will provide cuttings for next season.

Veteran chrysanthemum growers without glass have become skilled in erecting temporary screens of burlap or polyethylene stretched on sticks as winter protection for their outdoor flowering earlies.

The last batch of bulbs (other than tulips) can be planted. Drifts and groups are preferable to regimental lines.

Chinese lanterns (*Physalis*) may be gathered for flower decoration, and are best hung up to dry, top side uppermost.

Ruthlessly dismiss the dull and worn-out perennial asters, and order some of the modern, almost self-supporting beauties seen in the public parks or garden centers.

In the middle zones and to the south, dahlias can be lifted a few days after the foliage has been blackened by the frost. But if the ground is wanted for another planting, you need not wait for the foliage to discolor before lifting. Top growth should be cut down to 6–9 in. above the fleshy root and the plant carefully lifted with a fork. The fleshy tuber-like roots must then be laid out, stalk downwards, in a frost-proof place to drain and dry.

Ten days later the roots may be rubbed clean, and any damaged or doubtful-looking flesh cut away. A dusting with Ferbam, or Captan® is recommended.

Dahlias should be labelled and laid in boxes, lightly covered with vermiculite and stored in a cellar or frost-proof place.

It is now too late in the year to set out new plants with safety (except in the south), but the next few weeks are ideal for building a rock garden. Ground and stones will settle nicely before spring planting time. A good rule is to bury more of a rock than you expose, and to ensure that you have good drainage.

The orderly gardener will be anxious to tidy up the tired-looking border. The wisdom of cutting down healthy brown and withered foliage is debatable and depends on the local climate. Northern or exposed gardens benefit from the protection that dead material gives against cold winds and frost.

Dried ornamental gourds should be washed with a Lysol solution to control fungal spores; they should be dried and preserved by waxing or lacquering.

Greenhouse

All feeding of chrysanthemums should now stop; prolonged feeding is apt to lead to flower deformities and decay.

A final batch of viola and pansy cuttings may be taken and inserted in pots in a cold frame, or in a warm nursery bed outdoors.

Store hydrangeas in tubs or boxes at 40°F. (5°C.) in a darkened place (a cool room of the cellar is fine if some light is to be had). Keep the plants on the dry side until January.

Pot up Easter lilies and French hyacinths and store them in a cool dark place for root development.

Sow cineraria seed now for Easter bloom. Keep seed pans at 45°–50°F. (7°–10°C.) until the seedlings are ready to prick off. Keep the youngsters free from whitefly.

Glasshouse camellias and azaleas should be kept at 50°F. (10°C.) or a lower temperature at this season.

Abutilons plunged outside during summer should be pruned hard now, and softwood cuttings rooted from the new growth in a 50°F. (10°C.) temperature.

Vegetables

Lift turnips with a fork, taking care not to damage or bruise them. The tops should be twisted off and the roots stored in sand. Gardeners with a taste for turnip tops may leave half the crop in the ground and use the leaves as a vegetable.

Herbs

Cut down all remaining herbs to encourage young growth, lightly covering the roots with sieved soil. Kept warm and moist, plants in southern zones will soon provide fresh foliage.

Fruit

The last of the apples and pears should be gathered before the weather breaks or a storm brings them down. They can be stacked in deep, slatted boxes (up to two or three layers), and keep best in a dark, fairly moist but cool atmosphere. All fruit must be examined regularly from harvesting until used.

Clematis tangutica with enchanting deep-yellow lantern-shaped flowers and fascinating feathery seed-heads.

October
Week 4

Garden flowers

Now comes the turn of the tulips, and the gardener is advised to be adventurous in his choice.

There are the exciting viridifloras in unusual colors, with a splash of green on each petal: the elegant lily-flowered, the diverting fringed parrots, the multi-flowered types with three to seven flower heads to each stem, and the dazzling *Tulipa* species, such as *Fosteriana* scarlet 'Red Emperor', bright as a guardsman on parade, and its yellow counterpart, 'Golden Eagle'.

Lift the kniphofias (red-hot pokers) in northern zones, and store as for cannas in a cool dark cellar (see Week 1).

Planted close to the south side of a building and heavily mulched, they will come through most winters in zone 5.

One of the last clean-up chores is to remove and burn the decaying leaves from the iris. If the iris borer is present, and most gardens suffer its attention, the eggs are liable to overwinter on the plant. Leaf bases and old flower stalks should be burnt.

The borer attacks all iris, including the Japanese, our natives, and the related blackberry lily (*Belcamcanda*).

For earliest bloom in garden border or rock garden, plant clutches of winter aconite (*Eranthis hyemalis*) or the hybrid *E. tubergeniana*, a ground-hugger whose yellow flowers come two weeks before the Dutch crocuses. The small tubers are inexpensive. Plant them 2 in. deep, and mulch for their first winter. When happy they will self-seed and spread.

Sunflowers grown as a screen or for bird seed should be decapitated before they are fully ripe. The heads should be spread out under cover to dry for a couple of weeks before the seeds are gathered.

Indoor plants

The amaryllis (hippeastrum) should be at complete rest: repotting is necessary only every second or third year.

All tender subjects – the Indian azalea, Christmas cactus, solanum or Jerusalem cherry, and other house plants that have enjoyed a summer blow in the garden – must now be brought indoors again.

Greenhouse

A light, well-ventilated greenhouse, with a day temperature of 55 °F. (13 °C.), falling 43 °F. (6 °C.)–45 °F. (7 °C.) at nights, will suit the majority of plants. Slight ventilation may be given from 11 a.m. to 3 p.m. on sunny days.

Chrysanthemums: clumps of "earlies" that are in a frame should be cleaned up and leaves or branches of doubtful health removed and burned. Where this is not allowed, destroy them with the rubbish.

Another batch of perpetual carnations may be rooted.

Gradually cut down the water supply to fuchsias without letting them go dry. Treat the cyclamen to bi-weekly feeds of weak liquid fertilizer.

Bulbs of paper white narcissi, pre-chilled for forcing, can be started now in bowls of coarse gravel. Keep moist and in the dark for three to four weeks. Try a few of the lovely yellow 'Grand Soleil d'Or' with its attractive orange cup.

Ixias planted now will bloom in 10 to 12 weeks. Cover five to six bulbs in a 5 in. pan and keep in the cold frame under a foot of straw until December. Then bring indoors to a temperature of 50 °F. (10 °C.). Water regularly, and the lovely tubular flowers in a variety of colors will arrive in four to five weeks.

Most fibrous-rooted begonias sown now will bloom in March, given a temperature of 60 °F. (15 °C.). Try the F_1 'Scarletta'.

Bulbous iris planted now and grown at 60 °F. (15 °C.) will flower in February.

Vegetables

Store potatoes in a dark, well-ventilated, frost-proof place, remembering that if they are stored in heat they will begin to grow and sprout. Never allow the temperature to drop below freezing or their starch will turn to sugar. Ugh!

Winter squashes and pumpkins keep best when stored at 50 °F. (10 °C.). They might be found a place on a wide shelf or rack close to the ceiling in garage or cellar.

General

Gardens in the prairie states (roughly, Wisconsin west to the Dakotas, south to western Ohio and Missouri) often require more wind protection than the gardens in other areas. Windbreaks are the answer and local horticultural departments might be asked to suggest suitable plants to be grown in these difficult districts.

Reduce wind-blown soil erosion by planting winter rye over all bare areas of the garden and among the fruit trees.

Aster 'Carnival' adds a strong accent of color to the autumn border.

November

November is the put-to-bed month, and the farther north one lives the earlier it should be done. Most of the leaves have fallen from the deciduous trees in the woods. The winds can be cutting, frost crusts form and melt in the soil, and snowflakes fall in northern zones by Thanksgiving.

The roses seem to bloom a little later every year, early camellias now come into bloom in the middle zones, and the native witch hazel gives a cheerful dusting of yellow.

Snow is Nature's finest protective mulch. You may have been surprised at the number of different perennials hardy in the rockery and borders of the Montreal Botanic Garden (one of America's finest)—it is because of the depth of snow that blanketed them throughout preceding winters. I have seen plants thrive there that were winter-killed from southern New York to Cincinnati. A long-lasting snow mulch was the reason. Gardeners who cannot rely on this protection must provide the blanket for the less hardy.

Flowers are scarce this month, but the berried trees and shrubs, alight with autumn color, take their place.

Here, *Acer griseum*, the mahogany paperbark maple with dazzling red leaves, the yellow, orange, pink, rose to bright scarlet fruit of the mountain ash (*Sorbus* cvs), and the gorgeous flame of the sourwood (*Oxydendrum*) foliage, play their part in the garden. The accent given by a three- to four-bole clump of American paper or canoe birch (*Betula papyrifera*) is difficult to surpass.

Transplanting: there is always a danger when transplanting an old or long-established tree or shrub, especially this late in the season. However, if it has outgrown its allotted space, it may have to go.

To minimize the transplanting risk, thrust the spade down in a semicircle around the plant to sever outspread roots. The circle may be completed two weeks later. This treatment, which should be given several weeks before moving, will encourage the plant to make fibrous roots before it is lifted.

When lifting, wrap the root ball in burlap sacking or polyethylene, keeping as much soil attached to the roots as possible.

The plant must not be allowed to go dry at any time, and must be constantly watched for dryness during the following spring.

Set up the bird feeding stations and keep them well supplied with seed from now onwards so that the birds know where they can feed.

As soon as their favorite native seeds are eaten, many birds feed freely on insect eggs. The chickadee will eat 250 canker worm eggs a day. The nuthatch combs the oak trees for gypsy moth and other eggs, and during summer weeks the oft-scorned starling is a voracious consumer of caterpillars.

Hibernating insects are more likely to perish when the vegetable garden is forked over, plowed or rototilled in late autumn. Many of the pupae are then killed mechanically or by exposure.

Small fruit plantings grown on sandy or clay soils are improved by a rather heavy application of rotted manure, provided it is turned into the soil next spring.

November is a good month to add rotted manures to garden areas.

The relative merit of manures deserves clarification. They are important for the humus they add to the soil, as well as for the three essential plant food elements: nitrogen, phosphorus and potassium. A pound of well-rotted manure is higher in plant food than when it is fresh: most weed seeds will be killed during its decomposition. The analysis of well-rotted cow manure is 5.8-2-1.7; horse manure 4.4-2-1; and dried poultry manure 3-3-1.5. Litter-free poultry manure must be used sparingly to avoid burning tender roots.

The brilliant color of young acers (maples) in an arboretum.

November
Week 1

Garden flowers

It is getting late for planting daffodils, *Iris reticulata*, and the early bulbs.

Scillas should be planted in the grass and left to naturalize, and the yellow winter aconites introduced into the woodland.

Meanwhile, in warmer zones, anemones, either the single-flowered de Caens or double St Brigids, can be planted. Left undisturbed, they will increase.

Start dividing large clumps of perennial autumn-flowering asters and trespassing perennials in the border, but do not disturb the scabious or pyrethrums until April.

If the bird houses need painting, this must be done well ahead of nesting time; birds dislike the smell of paint. Color is immaterial, for most birds are relatively color-blind.

Indoor plants

Keep most succulents and cacti on the dry side until spring. The Christmas cactus is an exception and needs water and liquid fertilizer. But keep the plant firmly pot-bound.

Feed poinsettias with liquid fertilizer as soon as color appears in the bracts. Withhold artificial lighting in the evenings until flower buds appear among the bracts.

Shrubs

A generous quantity of mulch is needed in November (or by December in warmer zones). Power shredders (to be had on daily rental in many suburban areas) are helpful in preparing the mulch. A mixture, run through the shredder, of equal parts of deciduous leaves, healthy vegetable debris and fresh or rotted manure is moisture-retaining and nutritive.

The addition of superphosphate to the mixture costs little but greatly improves the product. Calculate the amount of material needed and make it up at one sitting. Warning: keep children well away from the whirring shredder!

Mound-mulch the buddleias to a foot or so high in zones 5 and 6, and prune them to about 2½ ft. from the ground.

Before mulching the roses, take a hand fork and mix two trowelfuls of dried cow manure, or one of Milorganite, into the soil around each plant to a depth of 2 in.

Hortensia hydrangeas (*H. macrophylla*) can be overwintered in the open from zone 7 southward, and in zone 6 with some protection. 'Blue Wave', the blue lacecap, is one of the best.

The very hardy Peegee (*Hydrangea paniculata*), with cream pointed trusses of late summer flowers, is an ideal shrub if you are on lime-free soil. It needs hard pruning annually.

The oakleaf hydrangea has brilliant autumn foliage, and offers white June flowers that turn to blue.

In southern zones, when the weather is mild and the plants dormant, the majority of trees and shrubs can be planted from November to February.

This is the favorite month for planting and transplanting roses. Plants introduced now have the opportunity of making good root growth before the severe weather comes, enabling them to make an early start in the spring.

The newly planted shrubs respond to a mulch that conserves moisture for roots: protection from severe frost is important at this time of the year.

Greenhouse

Partly open the top ventilators for a few hours during the day when the weather is mild, shutting them when very cold.

A temperature of 54°–59°F. (12–15°C.) during the day, falling to 45°–46°F. (7°–8°C.) at night, should be your aim.

All glass should be cleaned so that full light is available on dark days.

Remove the growing points of stems from the autumn-sown sweet peas, just below the second or third pair of leaves. This will encourage a short-jointed bushy plant.

The schizanthus must be moved on to the next size larger pot before they become pot-bound, otherwise there will be a check in growth.

Chrysanthemums are vulnerable to damp and mildew. Tweezers should be used for removing petals suffering from damping-off due to excessive heat or lack of air. An application of benomyl will restrict the spread of the disease.

Christmas-flowering bulbs can be discreetly forced.

Line the greenhouse with polyethylene to retain heat and save money, especially on the windward side.

To facilitate humidity control and propagation by cuttings, consider installing a few fog or mist nozzles on a ½ in. pipeline. Electric humidity-control valves are ideal, but a hand valve is much cheaper. Where the water is hard, nozzles require periodic attention to remove accumulated salts.

Crab apple Malus 'Golden Hornet'. The white flowers in May are followed by heavy crops of small fruit that remain on the tree until late fall.

November
Week 2

Garden flowers

A last batch of tulips may be planted, provided the soil is not wet or frosty.

Examine the dahlia roots and cut away any doubtful flesh, dusting afterwards with Ferbam or Zeneb®. If there is any sign of shriveling, the covering can be slightly dampened.

Sow seed of slow-germinating perennials, including most alpines. Set the aluminum pans or flats of seed outdoors, covering the soil with moist burlap, and mulch with leaves. The pans can be brought into the greenhouse in early March.

Lay down a 6 in. carpet of prepared mulch over much of the border, around specimens in the rockery, around all recently planted trees, shrubs and vines, and over plants known to be winter-tender. Ideally, this should be done after a soaking rain.

Some plants resent a heavy mulching, notably the biennial rosette-formers: delphiniums (for which an inch of coarse sandy gravel is better than mulch), foxgloves and hollyhocks.

Trees and shrubs

Roses can be pruned at any time while dormant. Whether to prune towards the end of the year or in the spring is a controversial subject. I prefer to wait until mid-February in the south and until mid-April in the north, when the sap begins to rise. But it should be said that gardeners who prune in December or January often get earlier and perhaps larger blooms than those who prune in the spring.

Whatever the method, strong, whippy growth should be shortened by a third in November to prevent the wind rocking the plants in stormy weather.

Mound the mulch around rose canes to a height of 12–15 in. on climbers as well as standards. Do the same for the clematis.

Half-hardies, such as cannas, hortensias and tritomas, need 8–10 in. of protection. Some gardeners prefer a pailful of coarse gravel over the crowns and under the mulch.

Recently planted broad-leaved evergreens, or those with obviously late or soft new tip growth, should be sprayed with a plastic antidessicant such as Wilt-Pruf or Foli-gard. Wait to spray until the temperature is 40°F. (5°C.) or higher.

Trees, shrubs and roses should be planted as soon as possible after leaf fall. In southern zones, planting that has not been carried out by the end of November should wait until the spring.

If the roots are dry, soak them in a bucket of water. Garden compost should be trickled in between the roots as you go, and the soil mark on the shrub's stem used as a guide to the correct planting depth. Having trodden down the plant firmly into place, level and loosen the top soil and mulch. Avoid doing any planting in wet or frosty weather.

Newly planted trees will require added protection, either from burlap stretched around stakes or pine boughs cut and arched over them. Cross ties will help to hold the boughs in place.

The nursery should be consulted as to the correct planting distance. Roughly, ornamental trees should be kept 20–25 ft. apart and upright growers and large shrubs at least 8 ft. apart.

Miniature roses should now be banked with a compost mixture, especially where snow cover is not reliable winter protection.

Hollies that have not berried well are probably either male plants or heavily infested with leaf miner. Make a point of checking the sex of the holly next May or June. If most flowers bear anthers, the plant is male and will remain berry-less. If female, spray regularly against leaf miner; also spray open flowers with a tomato or fruit-setting hormone to assist pollination.

Greenhouse

The temperature should not be allowed to fall below 45°F. (7°C.) at night.

Remove and burn discolored foliage from chrysanthemums to reduce the spread of nematodes.

Encourage blue hortensia hydrangeas to intensify their color by placing three pieces of alum (or special blueing powder) in the soil of a 6 in. pot.

Keep the camellias under 50°F. (10°C.) in the daytime, and avoid overwatering.

General

Control snowdrifts with slatted snow fences, fastened to $\frac{1}{2}$ in. steel rods. A snow fence set 5 yds. to windward of the border or rockery can often collect welcome snow mulch.

Where rabbits or field mice are abundant, they may eat the bark from woody fruit trees and ornamentals. Wire, or some other form of protection, must be installed at a height above the expected snowfall. Alternatively, the trunks may be winter-wrapped with repellant-treated or tar-impregnated paper.

House plants—Dracaenas, Begonia Rex, crotons scindapsus and Alocasia sanderiana.

November
Week 3

Garden flowers

Korean chrysanthemums may survive the winter in the border in zone 6, but they are safer lifted, boxed and placed at the base of a wall. Where there is likelihood of severe weather, they should be covered with coarse clippings of pine.

Identity records are too often lost. Replace missing and faded labels before you forget where you have put the plants. An occasional hour spent doing this job will be well repaid.

Shrubs

Broad-leaved evergreens must not start the winter dry, especially in the plains states where November is frequently dry or windy. Roots need thorough soaking before the ground freezes, and throughout the area a leaf-mold mulch should be spread over them. In so large a country no one can say in which particular week this should be done. You must be the judge.

Failure to water may not result in loss of an established plant, but it can defeat and kill one planted this year. It can also result in bud drop and the loss of next year's bloom. In any case, add the mulch and leave it there permanently. Most broad-leaves are surface feeders, and the roots will enjoy this protection.

Greenhouse

The early planted spring bulbs will soon be ready to come indoors from the plunge, first into semi-light and then gradually into full light.

Paper white narcissus, and its yellow counterpart, 'Soleil d'Or', are the earliest performers and will bloom in five weeks after planting. Bring the others into the light gradually after six or eight weeks in the dark, by which time they should have good root systems.

Once the bulb is making healthy top growth it must not be allowed to dry out, otherwise its roots will shrivel – a condition from which they seldom fully recover. This is especially true of French hyacinths and tulips.

The gardener must watch for any signal of distress such as "drawing up" through lack of light or excessive heat. Bulbs started off in a good soil mixture will not require feeding.

The support of a light stake may be necessary for the massive hyacinth truss or the wayward daffodil.

Bulbs in bowls for the house should be treated similarly.

The large potted plant, such as forsythia, can now be brought into the greenhouse and forced for early bloom.

Sashes can be lifted or propped up from the frames on mild days.

It is a mistake to cut off hot water heat in the greenhouse on a warm day and allow the house to get cold. It is far better to open the top ventilators and keep the atmosphere moving and buoyant, and you will find it cheaper in the end.

If thermostat-controlled electricity is used, frequent switching off is economical, but keep the gap between "on" and "off" to within 5°F. (−15°C.).

Cyclamen in bud should be fed twice a month with liquid fertilizer.

Sow pansy seed now for early spring bloom. Keep at 45°F. (7°C.) in full light. Feed in order to keep the plant growing without check.

Vegetables

Lift and store Jerusalem artichokes and salsify.

Have you ever eaten salsify in the same way as asparagus? It is good if you like it!

Cut the artichokes down and store them in a frost-proof place.

Parsnips are completely hardy and can be left in the ground, but the long roots are difficult to lift when the soil is frozen.

Fruit

Strawberry beds should be mulched with straw or any clean mulch, such as poultry or stable litter.

Fig trees espaliered or grown on walls in zone 6 may require protection. They may be thatched with branches of spruce, attached butt end up.

General

Set aside a pail or two of coarse pebbly gravel to be used later for bulb-forcing and for humidification trays indoors. Another pail of washed sharp sand (but not the crushed quartz used in some aquaria) set aside now can be used when making a fresh mixture for growing cuttings.

Set aside also a supply of straw or old hay (away from rodents) to use as added mulch when next January's thaw reveals lifted crowns of your favorite perennials. Better still, have a bed of mulch handy, should the winter be both cold and snowless. When Nature provides no snow mulch, another must take its place.

Acer palmatum, the Japanese maple that turns brilliant orange in fall. The perfect small garden shrub, given lime-free soil.

November
Week 4

Garden flowers

Late-delivered herbaceous plants can still be planted in middle zones and further southward, but to the north they must be heeled in and covered with a leaf mulch.

Pansies started in August will provide March bloom if lifted and set in a temporary protective frame with board sides and a sash or polyethylene cover. An eiderdown of 6–8 in. of unshredded leaves should be kept between the plants and their cover.

Shrubs

Tread in any newly planted trees or shrubs that may have been lifted by early ground freezes. Did you mulch them well?

Indoor plants

Azalea indica (technically all azaleas are rhododendrons) is a small shrub that flowers exuberantly when in a root-bound pot, where there is little room for earth. The plant must be watered generously, sometimes twice a day, or on occasion plunged in a bucket of water. Rainwater, rather than tap water, should be used when possible for this lime-hater.

The Indian azalea demands even warmth and a humid atmosphere, free from drafts; a hot stuffy room will result in stripping the plant of leaves and shortening its life.

Have a care when watering bulbs in glazed bowls or containers with inadequate drainage holes. After watering, allow the surplus water to drain away; never let a bulbous plant stand with its feet in water for any length of time.

May I remind you again to draw the curtains at night between house plants and the windows in severe weather?

Cyclamen flowers should be picked by giving them a gentle tug away from the corm. If blooms are picked in the ordinary way the snag left may rot back to the corm. Water carefully to the side of the corms.

Treat the cyclamen to ten-day doses of liquid fertilizer.

Greenhouse

Fuchsias are about to take a rest, but there are some plants that never become completely dormant. They will require less to drink but must not be allowed to dry out and should be watered as soon as their leaves begin to droop.

Tender plants in a cold house should be plunged in soil to keep the frost from their roots.

Stake winter-flowering begonias.

Prune the plumbago and oleander.

Lilies in pots may be repotted (remove dead bulb scales). The pots can be placed in frames until the lilies start to grow, when they should be brought into the greenhouse for protection.

Gloxinia seed sown from now until March will flower from May onwards. The seeds are minute; they should be sown thinly and pressed into the compost, and the pan covered with a sheet of glass. A propagation frame, and a temperature of about 61°F. (16°C.) will hasten germination. The seedlings must be pricked out carefully and the glass replaced over the pan.

Fruit

Pruning season is any time after leaf fall and before the buds begin to swell in spring (for grapes, make it a month earlier in spring). The objective is three-fold: to keep the tree open and free of crossing or competing branches, to remove diseased or damaged wood, and to keep the height of the tree down to reasonable size. Add a wound-protective paint to all cut surfaces that are 1 in. or more across.

Prune now on mild days and avoid the raw cutting winds of March.

If you are in the heavy snow belt area, where rodent girdling is more common, tie up a small bundle of 12–15 in. fruit tree suckers for spring bridge-grafting work. Protect them with a turn of burlap and leave them in the garden out of the wind and sun.

General

Clean fallen leaves and debris from all eaves troughs. Spring freshets flowing over their sides can wash out or ruin treasured plants beneath. All plants resent drips.

Outdoor hose bibs should be turned off and the hand valve opened. Drain from indoors where possible.

Birch trees in New England.

December

In all but the more northern zones, there is no reason why December should be the bleak, flowerless month that it so often is in many gardens.

There are a number of winter-flowering plants and here the Christmas rose holds pride of place. The sculptured white blooms of *Helleborus niger*, sometimes tinted pink, is a masterpiece, with interesting, hand-like leathery leaves.

The plant may be slow to settle down, but given semi-shade, a rich loam soil that does not dry out and a taste of manure in the spring, it will respond and should be left undisturbed. The green-flowered Corsican (*H. lividus*), with clusters of dangling cups, the plum and purple *H. orientalis* 'Atrorubens' and the 'Lenten Rose' hybrids of the same species are enchanting when seen nodding together.

Iris unguicularis (syn. *I. stylosa*) from Algeria is another charmer that no garden can afford to be without, but it is for warmer zones only. I confess its foliage is untidy, but the early lavender flowers that hide themselves in the tufts are beautiful. If picked in bud when they appear, resembling tightly rolled umbrellas, they will give a magic performance when brought into the warmth of a room.

This iris should be planted at the base of a sunny wall where it can stay undisturbed: it needs good soil if it is to flower.

Another must for the winter garden in zone 7 and further south is the climber, *Jasminum nudiflorum*, providing gay yellow sprays during mild spells from autumn to spring. This is a willing grower needing good fare, shelter and regular tying-in. Wherever temperatures drop at any time to 0°F. (−18°C.), it must be protected from the wind and heavily mulched.

And finally, in these same warmer zones, please give a thought to the winter heathers. *Erica carnea*, the mountain heath, is a low-growing and excellent ground cover. Cultivars such as the carmine 'Sherwood Early Red' are smothered in bloom from December to March.

I can recommend *E. carnea* 'Springwood Pink' and 'Springwood White', of slightly trailing habit, as suitable for furnishing a dull bank, while 'Celia M. Beale' is most desirable, being one of the earliest and largest of the whites.

Erica darleyensis (a hybrid of *E. carnea* x *mediterranea* is another group growing to 2 ft., and is seldom out of flower from November until the spring.

Fortunately, the majority of winter heathers will tolerate a moderately limey soil, provided they are given a diet of damp peat and a place in the sun.

Among the autumn-flowering shrubs, the native witch hazel (*Hamamelis virginiana*) will bloom from November into December. The heavily scented maroon and yellow *Chimonanthus praecox* (syn. *C. fragrans*) cultivar 'Grandiflorus', a relation of the calycanthus, grows well in zone 6 with protection, and even more generously further south.

Gardeners are often disappointed with the behavior of their potted spring bulbs and want to know what has gone wrong. First, did they buy from a reliable source? Was it a bargain offer?

Did they let their bulbs dry out after they had started growing?

Did they bring their bulbs into the light too soon, before the growth was 3 in. in height, and the bulb head out of the plant's neck? I wonder!

Lawns are now dormant over much of the region. With the ground frozen, the turf is more sensitive to being walked on than before, so avoid path-making.

In colder areas, it is safer to lay down climbing roses and to cover the canes lightly with soil. Figs may be protected similarly, until the main stems are too large to bend willingly (see September, Week 4).

Poinsettias: red, pink and cream.

December
Week 2

Garden flowers

Work in northern-zone gardens is pretty well closed down until the first January thaw.

Further south one may now be able to remove debris from the rock garden. Alpines, wherever they are grown, are particularly sensitive to any winter cover of fallen dank and matted leaves. Rosette-forming plants, such as ramonda, many saxifrages and *Armeria caespitosa*, may welcome a prepared mulch around them, but never over them.

Shrubs

Where the ground is not yet frozen, and if the season has not been drenched by rains, give the broad-leaved evergreens their last soaking of the year, especially the rhododendrons.

Southern gardeners will do well to remember, when cutting the red skimmia berries, to leave enough of this past season's growth to produce next year's crop.

Wherever the ground is frost-free, as in the southern zones, this is a good time to move young trees of holly, oak, crape-myrtle, pawlonia, pecan and jujube. If the soil is clayey, be sure to make the hole large and use some good loam and leaf mold around the ball and roots. Feed the holly with liquid fertilizer as soon as it is planted.

When evergreen boughs or clippings are needed for winter protection, only use those that hold their leaves, such as the pine or true fir. Scotch pine is excellent. Beware of leaf-droppers such as hemlock or spruce.

Saltmarsh hay or seaweed cast up on the beaches make excellent winter cover, and both are weed-free and cheap.

Greenhouse

Aim at a minimum night temperature of 45 °F. (7 °C.) and restrict spraying.

The majority of plants will be resting, so avoid high temperatures and do not flog them with fertilizer.

Begin cutting chrysanthemum blooms for Christmas and leave them deep in a bucket of water for 24 hours before arranging them in vases.

Beginners often make the mistake of bringing their spring bulbs out of the dark too soon; the shoots should be at least 3 in. tall and the plants brought gradually into the light and warmth.

Inspect the hardy chrysanthemums boxed for the winter in greenhouse, cold frame or outbuilding, and be careful not to overwater them. Wet kills more chrysanths than low temperatures. The plants may now be cut down to 3 in. and treated to a top-dressing of finely sifted loam, peat and a sprinkling of sharp sand.

For exotic bloom in March, plant a tuber of gloriosa lily in a 6 in. pot of a sandy mixture. Soak well, water ocasionally and keep in a temperature of 60 °F. (15 °C.) until growth starts. Water more often as growth progresses, and support with a 3 ft. stake or wire rod.

Fruit

Raspberry and blackberry canes that fruited this season are to be cut off at ground level and destroyed (not composted).

General

The Christmas season is at hand, and now is the time to consider whether it is to be a live Christmas tree this year. When locally grown, its cost, balled and burlaped, is not much more than the price of some tree cut and imported from the north country. White and Scotch pine do far better than spruce. A fir is more than twice the price of a pine.

Set the ball in a large pan, wrapped in a wet bath towel. A quart of water a day poured on the towel should keep the tree going for two weeks.

Plant outdoors as soon as possible, in a hole 6–8 in. wider than the ball. After setting the tree in place at the same depth that it was planted previously, fill in with a mixture of the original soil and a good potting compost. Buy a couple of bags of good potting mixture if needed; the tree warrants such care.

Christmas greens, the native club mosses and mountain laurel are often gathered in woods for decorative wreaths and garlands.

Plant collectors on properties other than their own should only dig up plants with the owner's permission, and then only if the plants are growing in abundance.

A good bastard file and whetstone are all that are needed to keep the blades of rotary mowers and most garden tools sharp. It is comforting, when spring unfolds, to know that the hoes, shears and sickle are sharpened and ready for use.

The large-flowered cineraria, a showy greenhouse performer flowering from December to April. Many of the bright-colored blooms are centrally zoned with white.

December
Week 3

Trees and shrubs

Have a care and a heart when cutting the holly for Christmas, and don't rob the trees or shrubs of their natural beauty and habit. Take the branch that won't be missed so that the tree is not disfigured.

Firm up the newcomers after the frosts, and see that the stakes are doing their job.

Boxwood will require mulching in northern zones, but keep the material a few inches from the main stems.

Stake any young trees planted this season to protect them against wind, ice or snow damage.

Many deciduous trees and shrubs are best and more easily propagated by hardwood cuttings, taken when dormant. This is especially true when it comes to named and special cultivars.

Take cuttings with two to four nodes each from normal and healthy growth of the current year (avoid suckers and stunted shoots). Tie in bundles of a dozen or more. Bury them vertically 3–4 in. deep in a trench of sandy soil, cut ends uppermost. Calluses will soon form. Plant out in the spring, in a mixture of sandy loam and vermiculite.

Plants suited for this drill include forsythia, spiraea, Japanese quince, wisteria, mock-orange, trumpet vine and many viburnums, but not *V. carlesii*.

While on the subject, some deciduous woodies propagate best from softwood cuttings taken in early summer. Among them magnolias, redbud (*Cercis*), tulip tree, ginkgo (from male plants only). Lilac and flowering dogwood cuttings should only be taken from very young growth.

Most softwood cuttings do best if the bottom inch is dipped in a rooting hormone containing indoleacetic acid such as Rootone. These preparations can be had at leading garden centers. Manufacturers' directions should be followed explicitly. Finally, crop the leaf tips, root in a sand-vermiculite mixture, syringe in the mornings and keep the cuttings shaded for the first few days. A top layer of sand will help to reduce damping-off.

Greenhouse

There is more going on in the greenhouse this month than there is outdoors.

Large exhibition chrysanthemum cuttings are best taken this month: perhaps I should point out there is nothing to be gained in taking them earlier.

I am asked so often to give the best times for taking chrysanthemum cuttings that I now give a timetable:

November. Varieties to produce large specimen plants.

December and January. Large exhibition varieties.

January and early February. Exhibition incurved.

Late January and February. Decoratives, late-flowering singles and pompons.

Mid-February and March. Early-flowering (outdoor) varieties.

April and Early May. Decoratives for dwarf pot plants.

Here are a few tips on taking cuttings:

The plants should be in active growth before making a start. If they are still resting, bottom heat and a good watering will wake them up.

Choose shoots of about $2\frac{1}{2}$–3 in. long, of moderate thickness, avoiding the limp, hollow-stemmed or pithy.

Cut just below a node or joint: insert $\frac{1}{2}$ in. deep in small pots or boxes of equal parts of sterilized potting soil (from the garden center) and vermiculite, adding a thin top layer of coarse sand to retard fungal infections.

After firming up, water thoroughly, using a fine spray.

Syringe with tepid water in the mornings when the cuttings show signs of limpness.

Primula obconica should be watered regularly and given a bright position.

Freesias and lachenalias benefit by a weekly dose of liquid fertilizer.

Cinerarias and schizanthus should not be overwatered and must be allowed to come along at their own pace.

Citrus mealy bugs that bedevil the cyclamen and gardenias and many other greenhouse subjects can be dismissed with a forceful soap and malathion spray or, better still, by daubing each bug mass with a Q-tip dipped in rubbing alcohol. Kerosene is equally effective, but concentrate on the bugs and not the plant.

General

If your Christmas tree has been cut from its stump and is no longer a living tree, make a fresh cut just before planting. Any stand used should provide for water, although some people prefer a bucket of moist sand. Take your pick of trees: firs are best for this job, but don't fault a well-shaped pine, which suffers little needle drop.

Perpetual-flowering carnation 'Arthur Sim', a cheerful 'fancy' bloom with distinct red stripes. An excellent choice for a cool greenhouse.

December
Week 4

Shrubs

Heavy falls of snow may break branches or spoil the shape of yews, camellias and other treasured plants, and should be gently shaken off. But ice-coated foliage and branches must be left untouched; the damage incurred by removing the ice-crusts may well be worse than any leaf scald caused by bright sunshine!

Tender shrubs can be protected with pine branches, or with a sheet of polyethylene. We usually get the worst weather in January and February, so care for them now.

Compost from the heap can be wheeled to the shrubbery when the ground is frozen hard.

From the more southern gardens, branches of yellow *Jasmine nudiflorum* brought into a warm room will promptly burst into flower.

Indoor plants

Hippeastrum bulbs (better known as amaryllis) potted earlier can now be started into growth. They make entertaining house plants, growing at a magical pace. Shut-ins gain much pleasure from these and children are especially fascinated by their quick growth and unfolding.

The modern hybrids are magnificent, bearing three to eight huge funnel-shaped flowers in colors ranging from pure white to pink or crimson, with or without peppermint-stick stripes.

The hippeastrum that has flowered should gradually be dried off and put in a cool place to rest until started into growth again.

Greenhouse

Conservatory plants should be returned·from the house to the greenhouse as soon as the flowers have faded.

If the temperature is high, the floor should be damped early in the day to discourage red spider. But if an infestation is evident, spray with Pentac or Meta-Systox®.

Pentac® is one of the best miticides for greenhouse use. It may kill more slowly than others, but it leaves a long-lasting lethal residue on pots, benches and structural areas. Red spiders crawl from plant to plant, so their feet and bellies will absorb this residue in the weeks ahead.

Clean pots and crocks, and scrub the seed boxes when the weather outdoors is forbidding. I use Lysol and a mild detergent in the wash water.

Geraniums, cinerarias, primulas and other non-tropical plants are happier in cool rather than hot temperatures. They resent dampness and excessive changes of temperature, such as warm days followed by cold nights. A 10°F. (–12°C.) difference is ideal.

Side growths from ferns may be removed and potted up individually. Use a soil rich in humus.

Stop feeding the perpetual-flowering carnations and avoid soft growth.

Primulas and lachenalias will benefit from very weak feeds of liquid fertilizer.

Fruit

Complete pruning of fruit trees. Remove all diseased wood and burn if allowed.

To deter tunneling by mice, stomp down any snowfall around the trunks of the fruit trees when it is 4 in. deep or more. Hungry mice will travel considerable distances under the snow, and when food is very scarce will eat the sweet bark from apples, quinces and pears before they begin to feed on the more bitter bark of peaches and plums.

Cut flowers

Now that Christmas is here, cut flowers and gift plants are our common concern.

What can we do to make cut flowers last longer? Ideally, cut off a fraction of the stems with a sharp blade when the blooms arrive and, time permitting, plunge them deep in water for some hours before arranging them.

Roses and chrysanthemums benefit by having their stems hammered.

Tulips have an unfortunate way of collapsing; they should be wrapped up in parchment paper at night to keep their stems straight and stiff. Always remove the white portion of the stem ends: tulips only take up water through the green part of the stem.

A tablet of charcoal in the water will keep it clear.

Commercial preparations are available to extend cut flower life although few are really effective.

Once arranged, top up the container every, or every other, day with tepid water.

The Christmas rose, Helleborus niger, thrives in rich, moist soil and should be left undisturbed. Its blooming time will vary with the season and the zone where grown (as late as March in zone 5).

Postscript

This is the final note of the year.
Of course, you have kept a gardener's diary,
a truthful record of your successes and failures?
May the successes be repeated
and the failures forgotten.

In making this book the author and publishers have been
greatly assisted by two outstanding photographers,
Harry Smith and Valerie Finnis,
who provided all the photographs except page 23 (Bernard Alfieri),
page 85 (Donald Merrett) and pages 97 and 115 (Winston Pote).
We are also grateful to the U.S. Department of Agriculture for
reference for the Plant Hardiness Zone Map on the back endpaper.

Index

Page numbers in *italics* refer to illustrations

This edition first published in 1975 by CRESCENT BOOKS a division of Crown Publishers Inc., 419 Park Avenue South, New York 10016
by arrangement with Octopus Books Limited
ISBN 0 7064 0414 9

© 1973, 1975 Octopus Books Limited
Produced by Mandarin Publishers Limited, 14 Westlands Road, Quarry Bay, Hong Kong
Printed in Hong Kong

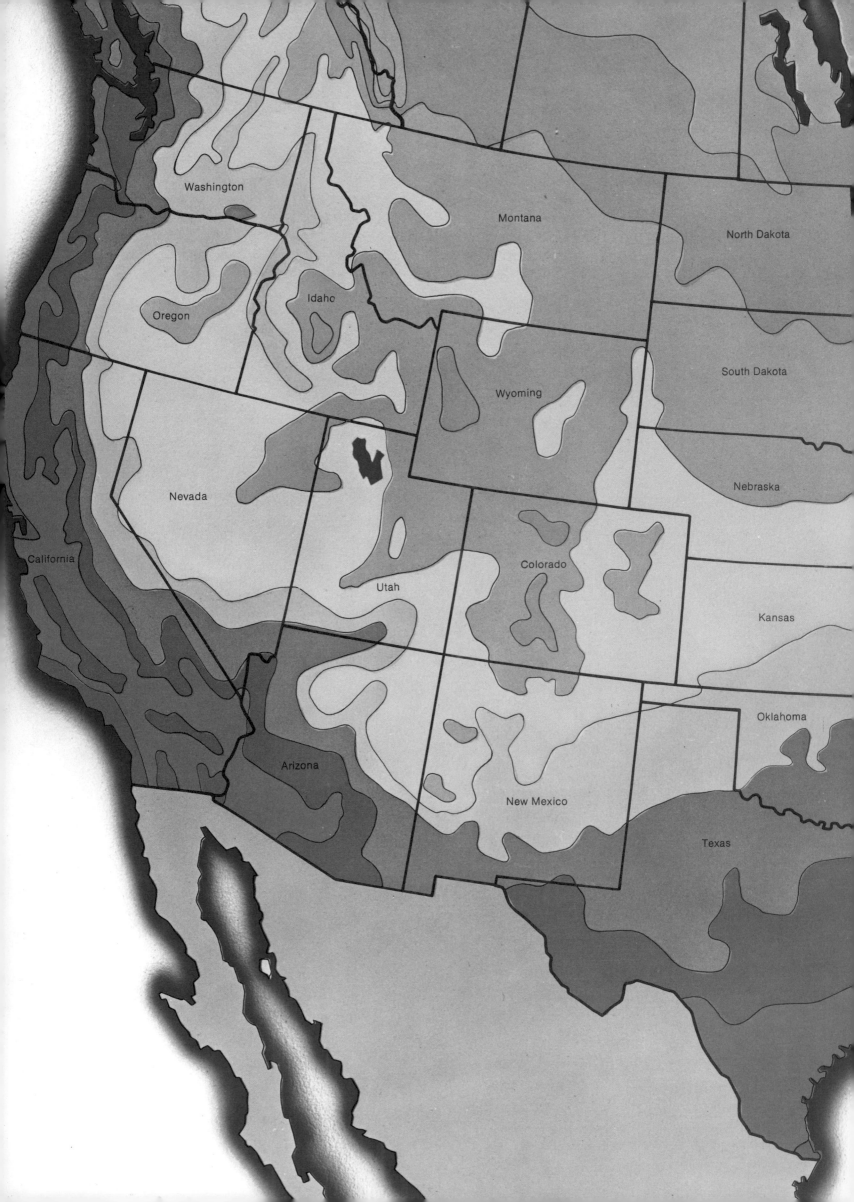